Trying to Catch Lightning in a Jar
Letters from Prison

I0521566

Trying to Catch Lightning in a Jar

Letters from Prison

Patty Prewitt

SOME
PEOPLE
PRESS

Published by Some People Press
PO Box 12453, Portland, Oregon 97212

Copyright © 2025 Patricia Prewitt
Cover photo courtesy of the Prewitt family
Foreword copyright © 2025 Barbara Baumgartner, Ph.D.
    and Beth Charlebois, Ph.D.
Afterword copyright © 2025 Aisha Sultan

All rights reserved.
First edition

ISBN: 979-8-218-68273-6

Cover and book design by Laura Glazer
Editing by Harrell Fletcher
Copy editing by Kristi Garced
Proofreading by Gretchen Dykstra

The image on pages xii–xiii and 196–197 are facsimiles
of letters by the author.

www.somepeoplepress.com
@somepeoplepress

Contents

A Note from the Publishers

Some People Press primarily publishes autobiographies by formerly incarcerated people who have participated in our weekly writing and publishing workshop at a minimum-security prison in Northeast Portland, Oregon. They work with us and their peers for over a year to draft and revise their manuscripts and, after they are released, we edit and publish their books with them. We have produced a couple of other books that didn't develop through the prison workshop (and have nothing to do with incarceration), but in those cases, we still had long-term connections with the work and the authors.

Trying to Catch Lightning in a Jar came to us in a very different way: Professors Elizabeth Charlebois and Barbara Baumgartner contacted us about a manuscript they wanted to publish, having found out about us from J. Malcolm Garcia, a journalist they knew who was familiar with our work and thought we might be a good fit. The manuscript was a compilation of letters written by Patricia "Patty" Prewitt to friends, family, newspapers, and politicians while she was serving a fifty-year sentence in various Missouri prisons. Patty had been able to type copies of her letters while working in the prison computer lab and had sent them to a friend for safekeeping. He showed them to Elizabeth, who had a student compile them into the manuscript that was eventually sent to us for consideration.

The first letter immediately grabbed our attention. It described the living nightmare Patty found herself in during the early days of her incarceration, being separated from her five children and experiencing the shock of prison life. The letters that followed, many of them sent to her kids, took on a different tone, one not of resentment, or even resignation, but surprising cheerfulness, as she made the best of an unimaginably bad situation.

Patty's writing reminded us of the work of popular humorists like Erma Bombeck, whose books, including *The Grass Is Always Greener over the Septic Tank* and *If Life Is a Bowl of Cherries, What*

Am I Doing in the Pits?, made wry observations about her suburban life, and Betty MacDonald, author of memoirs including *The Egg and I* and *Onions in the Stew*, which described her funny misadventures while living on a farm in the Pacific Northwest. Interestingly, both Bombeck and MacDonald endured horrible illnesses—tragic counterpoints to their lighthearted writing—not so different from Patty's excruciating circumstance of being imprisoned.

We agreed to publish the book, planning to work with Patty via Elizabeth and Barbara, as they were teaching classes at the prison where Patty was incarcerated at the time. But, in an unexpected development, Missouri Governor Mike Parson commuted Patty's sentence in December 2024. After thirty-eight years in prison, Patty was free. Not long after that we were on a Zoom call with her, experiencing firsthand the unique perspective and positive outlook from her letters. Patty told us, "I had no idea what to expect when I got to prison; I thought it would be horrible people there. I was sure I was thrown into a Sodom and Gomorrah. Then within hours, I found out the people in prison are just people, mothers, children—people in a bad situation."

This book covers the first eighteen years of Patty's incarceration. We hope to publish a follow-up book with letters from the remaining twenty years soon. Working with Patty through the editing process has been a pleasure. We are amazed that she was able to endure such a long and painful ordeal yet remain productive and helpful to others throughout. Patty's writing and story are not what you would expect from someone who spent decades incarcerated, and that is one of many reasons her book is so compelling.

— Harrell Fletcher and Laura Glazer,
Some People Press

Foreword

Patty Prewitt is as compelling in person as she is in print. We initially became familiar with Patty's letters in 2007, when Beth was on sabbatical from St. Mary's College of Maryland, where she taught Shakespeare and drama. During that time Beth served as the scholar in residence with St. Louis–based Prison Performing Arts (PPA), a nonprofit that produces plays with incarcerated actors in several Missouri prisons. Patty had been a leader and active participant in PPA since it began programming at the Women's Eastern Reception, Diagnostic, and Correctional Center (WERDCC) in Vandalia, Missouri, in 2005. A now late member of PPA's board of directors, Washington University Professor Emeritus Danny Kohl, shared the manuscript of the letters with Beth as part of his tireless advocacy of Patty's innocence and in hopes of finding a publisher. We are so happy and thankful to Some People Press that Patty's words will finally have a wider audience.

Even before meeting Patty in person, we started reading her letters aloud to each other in the evenings and were captivated by her story and the power of her voice. We learned that Patty had been convicted of the 1984 murder of her husband, Bill. After a sloppy police investigation and a biased and hasty trial, she was sentenced to life without the possibility of parole for fifty years. Patty refused a plea bargain and steadfastly maintained her innocence. The cruelty and injustice of her conviction was compounded by the agonizing separation from her five children, then ages eight to sixteen. Doubly devastated by the murder of their father and the incarceration of their mother, Jane, Matthew, Sarah, Carrie, and Morgan were raised by Patty's devoted parents, who drove their grandchildren the many miles back and forth to see their mother in prison and maintain their enduring family bond.

Beth's appreciation for Patty grew ever deeper while attending rehearsals at WERDCC, where she worked with PPA's now late founding Artistic Director Agnes Wilcox on a poetry workshop and a production of Shakespeare's *A Midsummer Night's Dream*, in which Patty brilliantly played the part of Bottom. Witnessing Patty in that moment, as she motivated a troupe of incarcerated actors and poets, while also reading, through her letters, about the searing trauma of her husband's murder, the legal travesty of her trial, and the early years of her incarceration—all over twenty years in the past—gave Beth a greater understanding of Patty's astonishing resilience and the excruciating nature of her plight.

After our first experiences with Patty in print and in person, we began teaching excerpts of her letters in our college courses. In both introductory classes in women, gender, and sexuality studies, as well as upper-level electives focused on gender and incarceration, our students were profoundly moved and outraged by Patty's story. One of Beth's students organized a petition drive and rally on the twenty-fifth anniversary of Patty's incarceration. Barbara's students wrote innumerable letters to Missouri governors and legislators. (Patty was in prison during the terms of eight Missouri governors before her sentence was commuted in December 2024 by Governor Mike Parson, shortly before he left office.)

Patty has motivated countless incarcerated women to make the most of their time behind bars. She became, and taught others to become, aerobics instructors and personal trainers. She recruited just about every actor and poet in PPA programs. In 2022 she joined Washington University Prison Education Project's inaugural class at WERDCC. Many of these women attribute the transformative changes they have made in their own lives, both in and out of prison, to Patty's guidance and example. We never cease to be amazed by Patty's positive influence on others, including ourselves.

This is a profoundly powerful memoir of the first chapter of her incarceration. A second volume will follow. We hope you find these letters as compelling and moving as we and our students have. The letters are both laugh-out-loud funny and heartrendingly poignant. They relate the brutalities, banalities, and absurdities of prison life and Patty's profound attachment and commitment to the people she loves on both sides of the prison wall.

One of the things that has struck us about Patty is that, despite nearly four decades of incarceration, her indomitable spirit has never been defeated by the deadening oppression and stultifying boredom of prison. There is something completely incongruous about Patty in a prison setting. She threw the whole place into relief with her laughter and vitality. Over these many years, she has inspired professors and poets, theater practitioners and politicians, legal experts and journalists, incarcerated women and Department of Corrections staff, who have become her advocates and, in many cases, her friends.

Patty's legal journey continues. Although her sentence has been commuted, she hopes to achieve the legal remedy she has long awaited: a full executive pardon for the profound injustice she has suffered.

— Barbara Baumgartner, Ph.D.
and Beth Charlebois, Ph.D.

Barbara Baumgartner, Ph.D. is Teacher Professor Emerita, Women, Gender, and Sexuality Studies Department at Washington University. Elizabeth (Beth) Charlebois, Ph.D. is Professor Emerita, Department of English at St. Mary's College of Maryland.

appreciable wet wea
such alone. The rea
re of home.

An officer marc
gruff gruffly asked.
I explained that u
it's raining. Unda
immediately go out
garden to toil!

Before I contin
that there are two g
INSIDE and OUTS
yard crew — inside
a building. Conf
Because I'm servin
I can never go
except in shackles

...so I'm pretty

...d sounds remind

...over to me and

...g I wasn't working.

...oit work when

...he ordered me to

...back gate to the

...I need to explain

...work crews,

...I work INSIDE

...force, not inside

...me, too, at first.

...so- parole sentence,

...IDE the force

...chains with an

Introduction

This is the story of the first eighteen years of our mother's thirty-eight-year incarceration told by her—through personal letters. As with life, some stories are absolutely hilarious, some are heart wrenching, some are informative, and some are unbelievable. All are true.

Our mother was serving life with no parole for fifty years for the murder of our father. She is innocent of the charge, and for almost forty years we, her family and friends, fought to bring the truth to light and free her. This is her reality. We only compiled the letters.

— Jane, Sarah, Carrie, and Morgan

Welcome to Prison

May 6, 1986

Life with no parole for fifty years. That's what my paperwork reads. I saw it in print the day I arrived. "Sentence: Life with no parole for fifty years. Charge: Capital murder." These pronouncements were boldly typed on the documents the deputy delivered when he handed me in. Fifty years. I can't come home for fifty years. The year 2036. I'll be eighty-six. Jane will be sixty-six. Momma and Daddy will be dead.

This is the first time I've ever started a letter with no idea who to send it to. I can't tell any of my loved ones the truth. And the truth is that I'm not doing well. My family always thinks I'm strong, but it's an illusion.

Since the night Bill was murdered, my life has been so strange and...and...I can't even come up with a word to describe my state. Everything has been off-center, overwhelming, difficult, wrong, insane, out-of-kilter, frightening.

I've been penned in this stark prison for nearly a week. Seems much longer and at the same time I feel like I just walked in. This is the first time I've been separated from my children for more than a weekend.

Dear God, what are they going through? Are they going to survive this? Who will take care of them? I love my amazing sons and daughters more than anything. My children are my responsibility. What can I do to make sure they are cared for properly? Loved enough. They have become orphans. Their good daddy is dead, and their momma is now as good as dead to them. God, what can I do?

I keep picturing Jane and Sarah's frightened little faces peering out of the back porch window of my sister's home as I was driven away from them in the early morning hours of that horrible day. The little kids were asleep, I believe. I can't recall. It's all a blur of emotion, pain, fear, anguish.

Why can't I remember? When events are too painful, it seems that I block them out—or they become fuzzy. Over twenty-five years ago I owned a pinto pony who escaped routinely to the neighbor. That memory is clear and crisp, but something as important as bidding my children a monumental farewell only a few days ago seems like it happened to someone else who merely told me about it.

We were allowed to use the phone last night. After our group was herded into a tiny office, the guard warned us to make our calls brief—no more than five minutes. I hadn't heard my children's voices since I was taken from them. When it was my turn, each of my kids talked and sobbed, sometimes individually, sometimes all at once—but the officer didn't stop me. I guess because I have five young children, she cut me some slack. In fact, I saw that she and all the others were also crying when I was forced to break the connection.

The kids are inconsolable. They wailed and bawled so hard they barely made sense. What can I do to help them? I can't bear their pain coupled with my own. Dear God, what can I do?

Let me focus on my physical surroundings. My emotional world is too soggy. But first let me think about how I got here. After I heard that my appeal was denied, my parents drove me to the Livingston County Jail so I could turn myself in, because my attorney misadvised us that I'd go to the prison there. Well, the Johnson County Sheriff Department declared that they deserved the right to drive me to prison, so I was transferred to them that same day.

The next morning, April 29, it took two tries before I was satisfactorily secure in the police car. After I was in the car the first time, the local newspaper and other media people showed up and requested that the officers take me back into the jail so they could photograph my shackled shameful sorry hobbled walk to the vehicle that was chosen to transport me back to prison. Happy to oblige, the deputies literally pulled me out of the patrol car and back into the door of the jail only to turn me around to retrace my steps—for the cameras. Guess "Take 2" worked for them.

Silently a grim deputy sheriff hauled me across the state to this razor-wired fortress of a prison, and once the necessary papers were exchanged, I was quickly taken to a big concrete block room full of steel bunk beds, army barrack style. A female guard led me to a small, not-so-clean bathroom—much like an old gas station toilet except for the addition of a rusty metal green-moldy shower stall.

I was ordered to strip naked and step in the cold shower long enough to get wet. She then poured delousing pesticide on my head while I was instructed to work the solution into my hair—both on my head and pubic area—and wait while parasites that might have inadvertently entered the prison on my hairs were eradicated.

I stood in the middle of the chilly room naked, dripping, and shivering while women piled in to use the restroom after lunch. Not knowing the greeting etiquette for such occasions, I smiled to each weakly in my shame and embarrassment. It didn't seem to bother them at all to use the toilet in the cramped room with the guard and me present. The poison burned my skin, and as I attempted to muster up the courage to complain to the officer, she thankfully gave me the go-ahead to jump back in the icy water.

The blue jumpsuit issued to me is big enough for my brother—men's size 44. They have no uniforms in a five. I wash out my panties, bra, and socks each night in the stained porcelain lavatory and hang them carefully on the steel bed rail. And each time I roll over in my fitful sleep, I flip my laundry, hoping to encourage the drying process. Each morning I put on the same damp underwear which are now marked with rust stains.

Mice, roaches, spiders, and mosquitoes also share this room, but they don't even bother me. I feel a kinship, I suppose, with these creatures of a lesser God. Unlike the rodents and insects I encountered in my free life, these little beings have nothing to fear from me—nor I from them. From the vantage of my top bunk, I watch them going about their business and silently wish them well.

Everyone in this room has a hard-luck story. Some tales are

pathetic, some are incredibly sorrowful, some are horrific, some are not true. My story? None of these women want to hear about Suzy Homemaker and how she ended up in this hellhole. Contrary to popular belief, prisoners do not claim innocence. In fact, they would scoff at such an idea. I'm so obviously a fish-out-of-water that I just keep my mouth shut.

I also know that if I mentioned that my plea bargain deals were offered by the prosecution and turned down by me, they would cuss me out good. And rightfully so. These women are so street smart. They never believed in the justice system, like I did. They always knew better. They were raised for the most part on the fringes of society.

Law-abiding ladies like me, who attended college, lived in neat two-story houses in the country, and drove children to games and dance lessons, are reviled, not revered. I did hear the rumor that I'm actually an undercover reporter doing a story on life in prison. If only it were true.

Last night we women of this room gathered on the concrete floor of the communal area and watched a made-for-TV movie about serial killer Ted Bundy. I realized that I am now categorized with him. Oh my God. Society now looks at me with the same revulsion and derision as evil murderers like Bundy. That sad fact settled on me like a thick wool blanket, and I feel heavy with the weight of the burden. Suffocating. Trapped.

Time to turn my underwear over again and lay down. It's very late. My bunkmate below me seems to have no trouble sleeping, but I don't want to annoy her with rustling papers and squeaky bedsprings.

Writing this has helped me feel a tiny bit more like Patty—and a tiny bit less like that brokenhearted, sobbing, stupid, wrongly convicted prisoner who's sentenced to remain in here for the next fifty years. Fifty years. 2036. I'll be eighty-six.

What is to become of me? What will become of my beautiful, precious children? I miss them so much that my heart aches with a pain like no other I've ever endured.

May 9, 1986

Dear Nancy,

So good to hear from you. Thanks for the sweet card. And, yes, I suppose Hallmark's selection of my-best-friend-went-to-prison cards is meager. Maybe a sympathy card would be appropriate. "Sorry for Your Loss"—the loss of your freedom, your family....

This prison is outside Jefferson City on the flood plain of the Missouri River. It's old. Very old. It looks like it might have been a military installation during the Civil War. The building I'm in is huge—two stories up and one in the basement—painted starkly white with a wide central staircase.

I'm locked up in a big room on the main floor with others who arrived recently. We're in a type of quarantine. The ones who have been through here before tell me that when we are "medically cleared," we will be moved in with the rest of the prisoners.

This prison will soon cease to be co-ed. We'll be shipped to a prison at Chillicothe, which is north. Didn't even realize both men and women were locked up here until a couple of days ago. Don't get out much.

Have you spoken to the kids? I'm so worried. I had the opportunity to speak to them a few days ago, and they are traumatized, as you can imagine. They are still reeling from the loss of their beloved Daddy. My folks don't know what to do.

Lots of characters here. One girl is only fifteen! She steals cars for "joy rides." She's young but her mental capacity is even younger—much like a toddler. Surely there is a better place for someone like her.

In the next bunk is a chain-smoking, whiskey-voiced sixty-five-year-old who looks 112 and writes bad checks on a regular basis. She's been here before and is a wealth of information. It's embarrassing, but I'm the only one who is not adjusting well.

My bunkmate is from Florida—a Harley biker who says heroin is her drug of choice. She showed me the track marks to prove it. I was in the clinic with her when they first drew our blood for testing. She and the nurse had a terrible time finding a usable vein and finally used one in her groin. Ouch!

The white-haired nurse is an inmate who looks scary as can be. Central Casting couldn't have found a better choice—one milky glass eye staring into space and the other glaring at the lowly newcomers. She makes Nurse Ratched from "Cuckoo's Nest" look sweet and kind. They say she somehow poisoned her husband with antifreeze. He was probably grateful.

Theresa has a dry sense of humor and swears this is not a real prison. The real deal is in Florida. This is "kiddie camp," according to my expert. A couple of months ago in Florida, while in shackles and chains, she gave birth to a son. Her baby was taken home by her husband within minutes of his birth. As tough as Theresa appears, or wants to appear, her baby is on her mind all the time. I can relate.

I have no idea what's going on legally. Don't even know if Beaird and Cardarella (my lawyers) know I'm here. One of the women told me that it can take years to get a conviction overturned.

This room contains a supply of well-worn paperback romance novels. I've read a couple of dozen already and know I could write them—it's a formula. Damsel in distress. Damsel meets a handsome tall dark/blonde hero but spurns him. Hero loves her when he sees her emerald/azure/violet eyes, long flowing raven/auburn/golden curly hair, heaving bosoms, arms akimbo, and tiny cinched waist. Hero saves her after much drama involving other men who are also immediately taken with her beauty. She falls for him. They are separated by horrific events. They get back together, fall into each other's arms. The End. Unfortunately, in real life it seems, no one rescues pathetic helpless ladies.

This morning I was sent downstairs to see the psychologist. Turns out there were two waiting for me, and they wasted no time on idle chitchat—not even a, "Hello, how are you."

This man never even looked up at me. He scanned papers in a folder, and mused as if to himself, "Hmmm...I see...well...I see she has no psychological disorders...hmmm...was a college student in good standing...excellent marks...hmmm...educated...skilled...no criminal history or tendencies...no addictions...hmm...."

He then shut the file and turned to the woman, "There's nothing we can do with her." The woman glanced at me and with a dismissing flip of her hand announced, "You can go now."

I guess that was my psychological evaluation. I left thinking those two have some sort of anti-social psychosis. Hmm....

Saw the most amazing tattoo yesterday. I stopped dead in my tracks in awe. A whole, full-color bald eagle is etched into this guy's back and arms. I'm serious. The wings are inked into his triceps. When he gestured, the eagle seemed to fly. Lots of body art in here. As it is with all forms of art, some is fantastic and some is god-awful.

Saturday, May 10, 1986

Dear Mary,

I have a job in the kitchen now—seven days a week. Mostly I work in the dish room behind plexiglass. When an inmate shoves his or her eaten-off-of tray through the opening, my duty is to grab it, dump the remaining food into a big trash can, rinse the tray with a rubber sprayer hose, and stack it on its side in a rack that travels on a conveyor belt through a contraption that's much like a miniature car wash. Steamy and hopefully clean trays emerge from the other side.

We stand on slippery wooden pallets—like the ones forklifts use to move squares of shingles—to keep our feet out of the standing water. The dish room is like a sauna, but it's honest labor and good for my wounded heart.

Instead of gently scraping the food off the tray, I've found that slamming it against the inside of the big rubber can is very effective—and feels good! WHAM! Therapy for my tremendous level of sorrow and frustration.

There are male prisoners here who fish for girlfriends. They write notes and wrap them around cigarettes as bait. Who in prison could ignore a free pack of cigarettes? They wink and smile suggestively as they slide their trays hopefully through to me.

And I let them see that I spy their offering of message-wrapped smokes—then, SLAM! The contents of the tray are splattered against the side of my slop can. I care nothing about their messages or gifts.

I only want to mindlessly and vigorously slap trays, and after lunch throw chairs up on the tables so I can swab the expanse of painted concrete floor with a giant string mop. I want to wear myself out so I can somehow sleep the sound, untortured sleep of the bone-weary. My goal is to numb the pain of my broken heart—if only for a while.

Sometimes the dish room crew is called upon to help the cooks with tasks such as prepping. This morning after paring knives were issued, we balanced on upside-down, empty five-gallon pickle buckets and peeled a mountain of potatoes. Keeping my opinions to myself, I only listened while skillfully removing their brown skins.

Sam, a brown-haired, bawdy woman sporting thick Coke-bottle-bottom glasses and a twisted roll-your-own cigarette dangling from her lips, entertained us with her version of the gruesome and senseless satanically inspired murder she had committed only a few years ago. I sat at her elbow and was forced to hear a story that would have turned my stomach only a couple of weeks ago.

But today I wore a poker face while I screamed inside, "I live and work in the company of women who are not only capable of the unthinkable—they have actually committed heinous acts of torture and murder. And feel no remorse, it seems."

Sam proudly spun her story like an industrious spider; I was caught like a helpless fly in her sticky web.

A few days ago, a pretty young Black girl with one gold-plated front tooth and dark tortured eyes quietly told me how she killed her baby. There was no pride in her telling. On the contrary. And my heart went out to her because it seemed that a lethal combination of postpartum depression and overwhelming desperation had caused her to make an awful choice. I was not repulsed or horrified. My heart was saddened that she had no support to prevent her from succumbing to her demon.

But hearing Sam brag about the torture and murder she committed froze my heart.

Monday, May 12, 1986

Dear Marsha,

There's a trailer house inside the fence of this prison, and somehow my family and I were ushered out there to visit yesterday on Carrie's eleventh birthday.

Mostly the kids clung to me and cried. A lady who works in the trailer provided a birthday cake and ice cream, which was so sweet, but this gathering was hardly a celebration. It was more like a funeral, as if I died but was buried in a prison instead of a coffin.

We hadn't seen each other since I left them, and we only wanted to hug and cuddle and be as close as physically possible. My beautiful babies with tear-stained faces jockeyed for position to be in my arms.

My Momma and Daddy's faces showed the strain of this emotional upheaval. They had not only lost their much-loved son-in-law and their oldest daughter, but the care and responsibility of five anguished children have suddenly been thrust upon them. As our "fixer," I know my Daddy feels absolutely helpless. How awful for him. Momma told the lady of the trailer about my trial and how I was innocent. Momma suffers greatly for the injustice of it all.

My eldest, Janie, is numbly doing her best to help her grandma with the little kids and the endless work required to meet their needs. Sarah's anger and pain is overwhelming and manifesting itself in the form of hives. Matthew, my man-child, feels much the same as his grandpa—desperately helpless.

Little Carrie and Bunky shared my lap, clutching me and sobbing—their baby-fine hair damp with the fever of despair. My blouse was wet from the tears of my children mixed with my own. Oh, God, how can you allow these precious children to suffer like this?

When we were told time was up, that we must go our separate

ways, the kids howled like wounded animals. My folks gently pulled the kids off me, and we did our best to soothe with promises that they would be back soon.

I watched as my family departed through the gatehouse and made their way to the old Cadillac in the visitors parking lot. Through the chain-link and razor-wired fence, my kids waved and blew kisses and motioned hearts in the air. I guess I did, too.

When they were out of sight, my knees buckled, and I collapsed. A couple of the girls pulled me up, I believe. I'm not absolutely sure. Don't remember the strip search or the walk back to my dorm.

Wednesday, May 21, 1986

Dear Mary and Jack,

If you notice, I have another change of address. Yesterday a vanload of us were hauled to a prison in Chillicothe, a town north of Kansas City. This prison is in the middle of a residential area.

Our free neighbors hurry to their vehicles, probably late for work. Yellow school buses pass by loaded with rowdy children. Birds brightly sing good morning. Rusty squirrels scurry about in their hunt for a nutty nutritious breakfast. The proudly blue expanse of sky has banished clouds for the day. Life buzzes on out there as if no one were in prison.

During the long ride here, the chatter turned to sex, and a boyish woman asked me, "Hey, you in the lavender. Do you play?" Judging from the gist of the conversation and her tone, I didn't think she was asking if five-card-draw was my game. Since I hadn't been involved in their conversation, I waited a moment and without turning from the window answered with a simple quiet, "No."

Undaunted, she continued on and explained that I would come around—and began listing the reasons. She droned on while with an aching heart I leaned against the window watching the people and animals outside the van enjoy free air—and the pretty country scenery fly by. I used to love road trips. Her part of the debate finished with, "So in time I know you'll give in and give it up, Babe."

I concluded the discussion with an icy glance and the truth, "No. Don't have enough time. They only gave me fifty years."

A welcoming committee of grim guards were gathered to help unload our van. Let me tell you, it's not easy to step, or rather leap, out of a van's side door with your legs hobbled by chains AND your wrists hooked with handcuffs to your belly by another chain wound around your waist. Perilous, but we all made it.

After we were unchained and while we were still rubbing the hurt from our swollen, bruised ankles and wrists, we from the van were herded into the back door of an old brick building. A thick, no-nonsense female guard who could have passed easily for a man took me into a small room containing a bunk bed and a small desk and ordered me to strip. I did. She asked that I raise my hands in the air while she looked carefully at my underarms and under my breasts. Then I had to show her the inside of my mouth and ears and toss my hair and spread my toes. But when she told me to, "Turn around. Cough and squat three times," I was stymied.

Putting my hands on my naked hips, I asked, "What? Do I cough three times then squat three times or cough and squat simultaneously for a count of three or what?"

Placing her workman's fists on her meaty hips, she glared at me trying to figure out if I was being smart, "Haven't you ever been stripped?"

"Well, yes, ma'am, but not in such a...a...choreographed way. I just took off my clothes."

"Well, this is the way WE do it. Turn around. Squat. Way down. Yes. Cough hard while you're down there. Yes. Stand back up. Now squat again. Cough. Squat. Cough. Good. Now bend over and spread your cheeks."

What? I had to turn around for more instructions on that one. Which cheeks? Oh. THOSE cheeks. Yuck. I've decided I really hate strip searches.

This morning the guard gave us permission to go outside to the backyard. Cautiously, I found a book and ventured out. I was leery because I had not been allowed outside except in shackles since my arrival in prison.

After making my way safely to the yard, I settled on a weathered wooden park bench and soaked up the friendly and familiar sun—trying my best to find my sea legs. I have yet to feel the slightest bit normal or peaceful.

The weather is warm, so I rolled up my jeans to catch the breeze and closed my eyes to say a prayer. Out of nowhere a guard appeared yelling at me, accusing me of "altering my appearance." Initially, I thought she was kidding, but, no, she chastised me loudly for rolling my pant legs to my calves.

Pointing her finger with her entire rigid arm, she ordered me to return to the dorm from whence I'd come—that is AFTER I'd rolled the legs down to my ankles. As I trudged back, she shouted after me, "Now you can roll the pants up IN your dorm THEN come back out here if you want." I stayed in.

I'm still wearing the blouse, jeans, and undies I came in with. We are clothed in jumpsuit uniforms until we are out in the general population. Once out with everyone, we wear regular clothes. My only problem is that I only have one outfit. My kind cellmate loaned me a nightshirt to sleep in. She says that there's a staff person here who has a basement room full of donated clothes. I'll find her and hopefully acquire some more options to wear. I also heard that there's a place called Clothing Issue that will issue me some panties, socks, and a bra. The ones I brought with me, and wash out every night, are looking sad. Oh, and this cellmate says that I can get permission to have a box of my own clothes sent from home. She called it a "home box," which only makes sense.

Last night right before lights out, I entered the bathroom armed with my loaded toothbrush. A tiny brown lady, dressed in a faded cotton gown with homemade rag rollers sticking out of her dark hair, occupied the first sink, so I politely headed for the second. She also moved to the second sink in front of me. Hmmm. I moved to the third, and so did she. We danced cautiously to the fourth and the last sink, then I stepped back to the third. You got it. She retraced her steps in time with me to the third sink.

During this encounter, I watched her in the mirror and now

have a face to go with the term "criminally insane." I'm searching for a word to describe the look in her black eyes and am failing. That's because, I just realized, there was NO look. There was a vacancy that gave me a chill. Turning away to the nearest shower stall, I brushed my teeth there and hurriedly returned unscathed to the relative safety of my assigned cell.

Today I watched that same woman regally sashay around the yard in worn plastic shower shoes dressed in a sarong of sorts over one shoulder and elaborate matching headwrap fashioned from green and blue flowered drapes illegally plucked from a dayroom window. It was as though this exotic costume of her creation transformed her into a stately woman of presence.

Lily is a Black woman of indeterminable age. She could be thirty. She could be seventy. She could be from a wartorn African region—a royal lady who's been witness to so much violence that she's retreated to a genteel world of her own making. The girls say she's from St. Louis and is just plain nuts.

Have you seen the kids lately? Momma and Daddy plan to bring them to see me Sunday. This all happened before the end of the school year, so I know they are distraught about changing schools and leaving their friends. I cannot quit worrying about them—keep seeing their sweet sad faces. What can I do? What a mess.

Wednesday, June 4, 1986

Dear Nancy,

What is it with prison psychologists? Another one called me to his office today, but he did make eye contact at least.

After I'd settled in the one empty chair across the desk from him, he opened amicably with, "Well, Mrs. Prewitt, how are you today?"

"Just fine, thank you."

"That's not what I hear. I understand you are depressed and cry much of the time. Do you want to talk about it?"

"Sir, I do cry. In the last two and a half years my husband was

15

murdered in the bed beside me; the murderer raped me; my five children and I were left to fend for ourselves and deal with all sorts of accusations, interrogations, harassments, and terror. I was charged with murder and in an incredibly unfair and short trial was convicted. So, I came to prison for fifty years and left my young, traumatized children in the care of my middle-aged, traumatized parents. On top of that, every time I eat a meal, my stomach knots up and feels like I've just eaten a fresh pack of double-edged razor blades."

After taking a deep breath, I concluded, "I think I have a pretty doggone GOOD reason for being on the BLUE side."

As he leaned back in his chair and ran his fingers through his thinning hair, he admitted, "Hmm...well Mrs. Prewitt, you do seem to have a valid reason for your emotional state."

Noticing his framed diploma read Rockhurst College, I inquired, "A good Catholic boy, huh? Hmm...I bet you're good and full of guilt. Wanna talk about it?"

And to my surprise he did. Nancy, that stranger unloaded on me for over an hour about his childhood, choice of career, marriage, fatherhood, and life in general. Hope I helped the poor man feel better. Sometimes it helps to talk.

Friday, June 6, 1986

Dear Nancy,

Mail call surprised me with a beautiful Precious Moments card from my mother-in-law. I've not heard from her since I came to prison.

In her little handwriting that reminds me of her son's, she wished me well and hoped I was bearing up and explained that her husband would be very upset if he knew she'd written to me. That statement weighs on my heart, because that poor dear lady lives in a prison of her own and is sleeping with her jailer.

She went on to tell me that the Precious Moments characters on the front of the card could be Bill and me—dark-haired boy and girl holding hands. She picked that card purposefully.

I want so much to write her back but don't want to chance placing her in jeopardy. It took much courage for her to mail this card. What if it had been returned-to-sender for some reason? How would she explain that to Bill's father?

Her heart is broken, I know. She lost her only son, and we never had the chance to mourn together in private—we two who loved him best.

But thank God, she knows the truth. The truth that I could never have harmed my partner, my best friend, the father of my children, my high school sweetheart. There's tremendous comfort in knowing that Bill's mother believes in me.

I just have to send her a note somehow.

June 13, 1986

Dear Mary,

Today definitely is Friday the 13th. This afternoon when coming back in from my job detail, I gasped to find a guard standing over everything I own. All my worldly possessions were on the floor of my tiny cell.

The bottom layer was my bedding: white state sheets and a gray wool blanket. On top of that were photos of my kids, their letters, and drawings—plus writing materials, toothbrush, and comb. The guard had poured out my bottles of shampoo and lotion, squeezed out my toothpaste, and scattered my stash of laundry detergent over the top—in the same way that bakers sprinkle powdered sugar over cakes.

As I stared frozen in disbelief, she stepped over the mess to exit and dispassionately offered, "Welcome to prison."

The Welcome Wagon is sure different on this side of the fence.

Sunday, June 22, 1986

Dear Nancy,

On Friday our yard crew boss came out to the backyard where we were noisily mowing and called my roommate away. I pushed a roaring machine while keeping an eye on Theresa as she walked to the building where caseworkers work on cases. There was something about our supervisor's demeanor that left me feeling uneasy.

Finally, I mowed close to him and asked where Theresa went. He didn't answer, but his eyes told me this was bad. I switched off my mower and stood my ground right in front of him. "What's going on? I'm her roommate. Don't send me back at noon with no idea."

Relenting he told me that her son was dead. My mouth flew open, "Oh my God! Which son? She had a teenager and a baby!" Our straw boss didn't know any more than he'd told me, but he did permit me to leave my job detail early.

Since she was my friend and cellmate, I feared the responsibility of consolation would be left to me. I was right. When I stepped into our cell, I found her on the bunk sobbing into her pillow, poor dear.

Quietly slipping into our one chair, I prayed she would be able to survive the shock. When she could finally manage to speak, she explained that her baby had died of SIDS. She'd spoken on the phone to her husband. The death was nobody's fault. Theresa only had herself to blame for being away from her infant when he needed her. That heavy guilt caused her to mourn with a vengeance.

We both mourned the loss of her baby boy—a son she'd never known. She also cried over the long illness and death of her first husband, the love of her life. I cried for the loss of my sweet husband, my high school sweetheart—and for my orphaned children. We cried for all our dashed hopes and monumental disappointments. We cried for wrong choices and lack of choices. We cried the desperate cry of women who are separated from their loved ones. We two from such vastly diverse worlds cried in each other's arms as sisters—in the kinship of the brokenhearted.

Thursday, July 17, 1986

Dear Jack and Mary,

Yesterday was a scorcher, and the yard crew mowed the huge pasture behind the baseball diamond. We marked off our areas and fell into competition to see who could finish first. Yes, it was crazy considering the heat index, but we were caught up in race-fever. Maybe we were temporarily insane from unrelenting sunrays beating down on our bare heads. Who knows.

Personally, I craved the feeling that honest hard labor gives me. And I've found that hard, sweaty work is as good as crying in the shower to relieve the pain of an aching heart.

So, our motley crew pushed heavy, thundering machines back and forth as we hollered and pointed out the fastest and slowest and laughed and sang—all our human noises drowned out by the roar of gasoline engines. We flopped on the sweet smelling freshly cut grass when we finished and good naturedly argued over who had finished first and who had had the biggest portion of the acreage.

That's when we were called inside to the Medical Center. The whole crew was marched into the air conditioning and ordered curtly to find a seat. Doris, an older Black lady who owns a salvage yard and sells drugs and other junk, mumbled, "Oh, shit. They gonna drop on us."

Everyone looked disgusted except me who was soaking up the AC and didn't know what "drop on us" meant.

Doris whispered to Trish, "Man, I'm dirty."

"We all are," I stupidly thought. "In fact, we're filthy! But what has that got to do with anything?"

Well, I soon found out that some vigilant guard had reported that we were acting strangely while mowing, so urinalyses were ordered for us all. "Dirty" means you've been drinking or drugging so your urine will not be "clean."

Since we had sweat so profusely, we were allowed to guzzle cold fountain water from cone-shaped paper dispenser cups. When it was my turn, the nurse took me to a not-so-sanitary toilet, handed me a cup, and stood there.

"I'm OK. I know how to do this. Thanks." I smiled so she could leave.

"Oh, no. I have to watch you."

"No, honest. I've had five babies. I can pee in the cup with no help. I've done it many times before. Thanks." Another big hopeful smile.

"No. I have to watch." Wearily she went on to explain, "You might try to adulterate the sample."

Guess I didn't look very honest to her, but I sincerely promised that I would fill the cup with no monkey business. I didn't even know how to adulterate anything. But she stubbornly blocked the door.

Recognizing a losing battle, I still could not bring myself to conduct my business in the presence of this stranger. "I don't know you well enough to urinate in front of you, ma'am, so could you tell me something about yourself? Please?"

So, she did. She's a single mother trying to manage on one income with an ex who shows up drunk and disorderly just often enough to upset the whole family.

I did manage to "drop" for her. And I was the only crew member who wasn't "dirty."

Turns out that Doris brews excellent hooch in five-gallon pickle buckets well-hidden under the old wooden planting tables in the greenhouse.

July 24, 1986

Dear Nancy,

The heavens have rained softly and gently all day. I couldn't mow this morning, so I sat under the shelter out back to enjoy the fresh warm summer precipitation. Prisoners don't seem to appreciate the rain, so I was pretty much alone. The sounds and scents remind me of home.

An officer marched over to me and gruffly asked why I wasn't working. I explained that we don't work when it's raining. Undaunted he ordered me to immediately go out the back gate to the garden to toil.

Before I continue, I need to explain that there are two yardwork crews: one inside and one outside. I work on the inside yard crew (inside the fence, not inside a building). It confused me too, at first. Because I'm serving a no-parole sentence, I can never go outside the fence except in shackles and chains with an armed guard. The girls who work on the outside yard crew are leaving prison soon—in the next year or two. They figure they're at much less risk to scurry away.

While attempting to explain to the guard that I should not go out the back gate, he belligerently cut me off yelling, "Lady, I'll hear NONE of your sorry excuses for being lazy. GET OUT THERE NOW, OR THERE WILL BE HELL TO PAY! YOU STUPID FUCKIN' BITCH!"

I was far outside the perimeter fence and wet with warm summer rain while bent over busily pulling weeds around the cabbage plants when my boss's boots appeared in front of me. Two whole rows were now clean as whistles. I straightened up to see his bug-eyed panicked face. "What the HELL are you doing out here?" he whispered harshly. I quickly explained what the guard had said and done.

In no time at all, I was safely back inside the razor-wired fence, and my boss was cussing out the numbskull guard who had sent me out. There WAS hell to pay—but the smart-mouth guard paid it.

Wednesday, August 13, 1986

Dearest Janie, Sade, Matt, Carrie, and Bunky,

You won't believe this, but one of the members of the yard crew is EXACTLY Janie's age! I almost fell over!

Cheri's curly copper-colored ponytail bobbed merrily as she told us that today is her birthday. I exclaimed that today is also my oldest daughter's birthday, my firstborn baby girl.

Then she told me she turned seventeen today. My mouth flew open. "You were born in 1969?" She was. Cheri and Janie came into this world on the very same day! And Cheri is in this horrid prison with me instead of enjoying the summer vacation before the start of her senior year. Oh my God. Poor baby.

Pulling me aside, Cheri told me some of her story. She's serving a twenty-five-year sentence for second-degree murder because she was sitting in the car unwittingly waiting for her boyfriend to pick up his paycheck. Or so she thought. He murdered his employers instead. After he informed Cheri of what he'd done and threatened her if she told, she went about her days trying to function like a normal fifteen-year-old—until the truth came out.

Cheri never had the opportunity to earn her driver's license. She will not go to the prom or attend her high school commencement. She's not researching which college to attend. She's not spending the weekend at a slumber party chattering about boys, concerts, school, and future plans, and eating delivery pizza. This sweet, intelligent, fun-loving, pretty little girl who's exactly Jane's age will grow up in this strange environment away from her parents and siblings. All this because of a rotten choice.

Do you see the moral to this story? You know I'm not writing this just to entertain. Little redheaded, freckle-faced Cheri is a good person from a good family. She made a wrong choice that has adversely affected the course of her entire life—and adversely affected her loved ones too, as you well know. When someone goes to prison, the whole family pays.

Please choose your friends carefully. Choose your activities carefully. Life is all about choices. I want so much for you all to live wonderful lives. That's why I tell you about the girls I meet in here—so you can see the disastrous results that come from poor choices.

I love you more than I can ever express—and I'm so proud of each of you. You're wonderful and special. I can't wait to get my hands on you. Cheri is looking forward to meeting you all. Her folks are coming to visit on Sunday, too.

September 15, 1986

Dear Mary,

Beaird came to see me today. Evidently, he had been here for quite a while before I was located digging up a flower bed behind a dorm. Wouldn't you think that security would be a tad more concerned when a dangerous felon such as me can't be found? But nobody got excited.

We meet with attorneys across the street in the administration building, and I was instructed to walk over there alone while the front gate guard monitored. I can't tell you how weird it felt to be outside the fence in the relatively free world. I stopped in the middle of Third Street and looked around. The world does look different out there.

When I made my way into the administration building, a sour receptionist looked me up and down as if I had carried dog poop in on my shoes, then led me to a conference room. There I found Bob all decked out in legal-eagle gear: freshly shaven and shorn, nice dark suit and distinguished tie, leather briefcase, yellow legal pad, and gold-trimmed pen.

I wanted to know what was going on legally, and he wanted to know what I was up to. So, I quickly explained to him that I had enrolled in a business school called Platt Junior College. I take classes for half a day and work yard crew in the afternoon. I am also taking evening college classes offered by Trenton Junior College. (I not only love learning, I want to be a role model for my children. Our children look at what we DO—not what we SAY we do.) Oh, and I added that in my "free" time, I teach art classes for Recreation and am an editor for the prison newsletter.

Bob's report was not nearly so clear-cut or promising. He lectured that winning an appeal is much like trying to catch lightning in a jar. I pictured myself standing on a hill during a wild electrical storm with the wind and rain whipping and thunder rolling over me—while I hold a mason jar high in the air, hoping lightning will strike so I can capture a bolt and thus go home.

As Beaird droned on, my heart felt heavier and heavier—and

23

the movie in my mind of me returning triumphantly to my folk's ranch and scooping up my wildly ecstatic children became dimmer and dimmer.

Mary, I'm so scared. Beaird said that innocence is the worst defense, but it's the only one we have. What can I tell the kids? They have their hopes up so high. I can see that in many ways they are just treading water waiting for me to come back home so they can resume their normal lives. I need to help them move on without me—somehow.

September 30, 1986

Dear Nancy,

My sweet folks bring the kids to see me nearly every Sunday, and we play games out in the courtyard between the dorms.

Recently I discovered that bunches of ladies in both dorms love to watch us play. They press their noses against the windowpanes to enjoy the Prewitt Family Show. The girls who live on the wrong side of the halls crowd into the laundry rooms to get a glimpse.

Several have asked me what we play, but when I tell them Simon Says, Statue, Red Light/Green Light, they have never heard of these games. Isn't that strange? Is it a cultural gulf?

We've started a visit tradition because the kids want individual private time with me. I take one child at a time to a far park bench out of earshot. Sometimes the kids rat on each other, but now and then there's a real problem involving growing up, school, relationships, rules....

These talks are very dear to me. I want to always be there for them emotionally—since physically is impossible now. I want to know what's going on in their little heads and big hearts. They must always know that my love for them is unconditional and never-ending. No matter what.

My nieces and nephews ask to participate in these one-on-one sessions, too. The kids take them very seriously, which is so endearing. Before they get here, they must ponder what their topic will be. Not one has ever walked back to the bench with me and had nothing to ask or report.

None of them have any idea what a joy and pleasure it is to look into each beautiful solemn face and hear each childish concern—and to be able to reason and hug away the fears. Most of the time.

Last visit Bunky and I spoke, he asked, as he held my face with his pudgy little-boy hands that smelled of M&M's, "Mommy, do you have fifty years?"

His beautiful dark eyes searched my face with so much intensity I could feel my tears well up and my chest tighten. I didn't want to tell him the truth. He's had so much to deal with during his nine years on this earth. Aren't we mothers supposed to protect our offspring?

But Bunky already knows the answer. He asked it so I would fix it like I do the other problems.

Hugging him close to me, I answered softly, "Yes, Bunk, but we're working on it. We're working hard to change that, so I'll be able to come back home to you."

"Mommy, when you were home, we had ice cream bars every day."

"Honey, it only SEEMED like we had ice cream bars every day."

"Well, we had fun every day, Mommy," he pointed out sadly while he snuggled in closer so I could stroke his soft hair.

"That we did, sweetheart. That we did."

Sunday, October 26, 1986

Dear Mary and Jack,

One of my neighbors appeared at my door today, and with big, panicked eyes asked urgently, "Patty, please keep Mr. M busy. I need a diversion BAD."

Easily I found an excuse to engage the dorm officer in conversation. He loves attention and the chance to express his opinions on anything.

As the lonesome guard and I chatted, the strong aroma of yeasty rotten fruit engulfed us. Dutifully I kept him focused, because inherently I knew that awful odor had something to do with the emergency. Thankfully, Mr. M noticed nothing. He was too engrossed in telling a story to this captive, if not captivated, audience.

It turned out that Garland was making hooch in her room—in one-gallon plastic mayonnaise jars—and had failed to burp the batch on time. The jars had exploded with the pressure of inattention—and the girls in that four-man room were feverishly mopping up half-brewed cocktails.

When the mess was cleaned up, Garland gave me the all-clear sign behind the guard's back, I extracted myself from the conversation, and life went back to the normal prison buzz.

I'm sure Garland will have a new batch going soon. She's a dedicated drinker. In fact, I heard she's been drinking hair spray.

She doesn't drink it straight. She filters it through fabric to remove some of the glue. Fingernail polish is not safe around her either. That CAN'T be good for a body.

November 30, 1986

Dear Nancy,

I hate that my family and friends must come to this dreadful place and are treated like second-class citizens just to see me. Some of the staff act like these good, solid, law-abiding citizens who love me are the criminals.

Sunday when Momma, Daddy, and the kids came to visit, Daddy wanted to tell me what they'd bought the kids for Christmas, but of course he didn't want the kids to hear. Daddy loves playing Santa—and Momma is an early bird shopper.

Daddy pulled me closer so he could whisper in my ear, and I perched on his knee as he quietly and proudly listed the big major gifts.

The visiting room guard exclaimed loudly, "OH, MY GOD!

WHAT ARE YOU DOING? YOU KNOW BETTER THAN THAT!"

I slid off Daddy's knee as he quietly answered, "I'm talking to my daughter. That's all."

"Well, don't EVER let me catch you sitting on his lap again. We won't have that going on in here!"

I could tell Daddy was horribly embarrassed. I sure was. But he looked her right in the eye and pronounced, "Your father must have been a horrible person."

If the proverbial pin had dropped, we would have heard it. Everyone in the room was stunned and wondered if the witch might whirl around and turn Daddy into a frog or something.

But she only snorted, turned on her heels, and tromped away. I need to keep an eye on her though. She won't easily forget that.

December 15, 1986

Dear Nancy,

I never did like writing in pencil. In fact, I KNOW you've never received a letter from me that wasn't written in ink. There is only one reason that this particular letter is penciled, and that's because I'm in the hole. (We call it the hole, but it's actually just a cell. Maybe it's a hole in the wall?)

Anyway, I'm in solitary for punishment. I was escorted here yesterday directly after Momma, Daddy, and the kids left. As with all good stories, it's a long one—and I have the time to tell it. Let me begin at the beginning.

In August we were informed that the law now allowed for male guards to pat search us. "Cross-gender pat search" is the technical term. Male staff had been forbidden until then. You've probably seen frisks on cop shows on TV. It's just like that. To "assume the position," we stand with our back to the searching officer with legs apart and arms outstretched. The guard then runs his/her hands over our breasts, buttocks, arms, legs, between our legs, attempting to feel for contraband. I've yet to see an officer find anything of interest, but they search as they might.

As soon as the ban was lifted, one guy took full unabashed advantage. As a friend and I exited the dining room, he motioned for Carol to assume the position in front of him. I watched in horror as he reached around, cupped her breasts, and squeezed and squeezed and lightly bounced them.

Like the good friend I am, I slipped away from the scene of the crime as fast as my skinny legs would carry me—and hid at the top of the stairs waiting for Carol. Since I hadn't stuck around to see the whole humiliating mugging, I don't know what more he did to her, but she was white as a ghost when she topped the stairs—so shaken that she was speechless and trembling.

Carol is sweet and articulate, a very nice woman with two almost-grown daughters. To land in prison, Carol had run a sedan over her abusive husband while he tried to yank her out of the car and kill her. She's serving twenty-five years for second degree murder with a three-year armed criminal action charge tacked on the end.

The guard's blatant disregard for her already bruised feelings and this outright sexual assault had just about pushed her over the edge. The federal court that had loosed the male guards on us hardly had this in mind.

Since we're lowly inmates, there was no recourse. We grumbled to each other, but we couldn't really DO anything. Prison days rolled on. We heard horror stories about this guard and his searches, and we all did our best to steer clear of him—to the point that some of us will miss meals if we see that he's on chow duty. You KNOW it's a problem if I miss a meal.

Well, yesterday I was called to the visiting room to see my sweet folks and the kids. Lurking outside the room was the guard. He leered, "Over here," while he motioned for me with big beefy sweaty paws.

I just could not do it. Politely I suggested that the female officer who was standing right there conduct the pat search. Since I didn't jump right into his arms, he instantly became mad as a wet hen. Perverts do NOT like their prospective victim to balk.

He loudly ordered me to him. The veins were sticking out on his meaty, thick red neck. My legs would not move. The rational part of me knew that I was in big trouble. The hurt little girl in me couldn't allow him to touch me.

I whispered plaintively, "Please, sir, I'm a rape victim. I beg you to allow the female guard to search me." The heat of shame rose to my cheeks. My vulnerability and the fact that I refused to comply only poured coals on the fire of his anger.

Oh, I forgot to tell you that my family was watching the entire exchange. I glanced over to see their anxious faces. They had no idea what was going on but could tell it was not good. Daddy's jaw was set. I had seen that look before—like when a steer refused to cooperate. Seeing his face reminded me of the kind of people from whom I come and turned my trembling fear into steely mule-headedness. And you know I can plant my hooves when push comes to shove.

Trying to sound like a grown-up who's in charge, I sternly advised, "If you're not going to allow me to visit, give my family the big box of Christmas gifts that I made for them. The box is in the property room in the basement. Do you understand?"

By this time every husband in the visiting area was asking his wife if that particular greasy-headed fat man had run his hands over her. I was not alone in my indignation and could feel the energy shift. My mind was made up. I would lose my visit before I would allow that letch to fondle me.

The two guards exchanged looks and came to the conclusion that the female would search me and that I could have my visit. As I entered the visiting room, my kids jumped on me hugging and crying—clinging to me. The husbands in the room glared at the male guard and offered low threats. It's really not uncommon for husbands to take exception to other men fondling their wives.

I enjoyed my Christmas visit and this small victory for several hours. But as soon as my family hugged and kissed me goodbye, I was pulled aside from the rest of the inmates and curtly informed that I was going to the hole for "creating a disturbance and disobeying a direct order."

The story doesn't end there. As that same male guard escorted me out of that building to the hole, we saw a crowd of people standing at the front door of the superintendent's house. The warden resides directly across the street from the prison in a house that's attached to the administration building.

I asked the guard, "Who's that?" Before he could answer, I realized that the group consisted of my family and every visitor! The officer answered dully, "Probably some sort of religious folks."

Sarah spotted me, and the whole crowd turned to witness and cheer for me during my march to solitary. Waving at my champions across the tall razor-wired fence, I stepped in time with the disgruntled guard to the disciplinary segregation unit. The sweet act of rebelliousness from the other side of the wire eased my wounded heart and caused it to ache all at once. No matter what these prison people do to me, I know I will survive because of my loved ones.

So here I sit on this steel bunk in this tiny bare cell, alone with some paper, a nub of a pencil that must be sharpened by the guard, and my thoughts and prayers.

Wonder if I'll spend my very first locked-up Christmas in solitary? Doesn't matter. Christmas won't be with my loved ones either way.

March 23, 1987

Dear Nancy,

Notice this is written in pencil? Yep, I'm back in the hole.

Remember that disgusting guard who wants to pat search me? I avoid him like the plague, but yesterday he was lurking outside the dining room picking likely females to fondle in the name of security. When I glimpsed his mug, I took a deep breath and attempted to slip out unobtrusively behind an obese older woman. He does not search every "body" who walks past him. He's choosy.

Of course he spotted me, "Hey, Prewitt. Over here." With a sinking heart and narrowed eyes, I slowly stepped the few feet to him.

"Turn around," he barked. "I AM going to search you today, honey."

Another deep breath to go with my mule impression. "No, sir. You're not. I request the female officer." Can you imagine throwing scalding water on a wildcat? That was his reaction.

To make a long story short, I'm back in the hole. My life would be much easier if I could just back up to that guard's fat belly, feel his hot panting breath on the back of my neck, and take his sexual abuse. But I cannot bring myself to do that.

If this were happening 100 years ago, I would be willing to take my punishment from a bullwhip. That's how stubborn I am about this. But it's 1987. Prison reform dictates that I be segregated from prison society. I'm not fit to mingle with the worst women in Missouri.

Don't worry about me. The hole is not too bad. I get "three hots and a cot." You'd think that solitary would be quieter, but a couple of the patrons up the hall like to voice their dissention loudly. Their stamina is astounding.

While I was in the hole at Christmas, my friend Carol spoke to the major concerning my plight. He simply told her that I needed to learn to conform. I needed to learn that there was no use in fighting prison rules. A few of us are thinking about filing some sort of suit about this. Surely this type of treatment is a violation of our civil rights—whatever rights we may have left in this uncivil place, besides our right to remain silent. Anyway, the major is correct. I have not learned to conform.

Just remembered how I amused myself during my last hole stay. My sister had sent me a musical Christmas card with a tiny light at the top of the glittered Christmas tree. The officer's post is outside our cell block, so after he locked us in, I opened the card. Computer-chip-generated carols tinkled merrily.

Hearing keys in the lock, I quickly closed the card and shoved it under my mattress. He went from cell to cell looking for the source of the music. Scratching his head, he left the area and locked the gate. I fished the card back out and opened it again. Yep, I heard keys in the lock. I did it over and over through every shift. Cracked me up!

Also, after lights out, I danced the card around the exterior window so that the "yard guard" could see the miniature light. He stopped dead in his tracks and squinted. UFO? Then he radioed the segregation guard who was busy trying to unlock the gate to investigate the music.

The hardest part was playing dumb when the flashlight was aimed in the tiny window of my cell door. "Hey! What's going on? I'm trying to get some shut-eye here...."

It's All Just Live Entertainment

April 29, 1987

Dearest Janie, Sade, Matt, Carrie, and Bunky,

Today's the anniversary of the day I left you kids. Not anything to celebrate, is it? I need to apologize for the lack of planning. I was the Queen of Denial, because I honestly never thought I'd have to leave you. Therefore, I didn't plan ahead as to where you kids could go if I was snatched up and sent to prison.

This last year has been so difficult for you—uprooted from the familiarity and safety of your community and school. It all breaks my heart, and I pray to God that I can make this up to you soon.

Wanna hear a funny prison story about a resourceful prison character? Joyce is an elderly lady, and by the way she speaks, she has had an education and good upbringing. She's no dumbbell. But she is odd as can be.

The first and strangest aspect of Joyce that the casual observer will notice is her cosmetics use. She creatively uses cigarette ashes, art supplies, and food to create makeup and hair color. Yep. Since I work as a recreation volunteer, Ms. J has warned me to keep an eye on the magic markers, colored pencils, and paint that we check out for arts and crafts projects. Joyce will "cuff" a marker in a split second.

Her hair is absolutely white, but no one would know it, because she mixes up a dark gray-brown pasty concoction of ashes and paint to color her hair. She wears it in a rat's nest and touches up the roots periodically—but NEVER washes the mess. In fact, she never bathes—period. Water messes up the masterpiece. So, you can imagine she carries a strong and distinct odor described as "funky" by many in here.

Her eyebrows are drawn on with colored and/or grease pencils—and her eyeliner is the same, but usually a different color—she favors blue. Her lips and cheeks are rouged with Kool-Aid she steals from the kitchen. Joyce even applies bright eyeshadow of her own making. She's a sight to behold, like a demented clown might appear in a Freddy Krueger movie.

Do you kids want to know how I know her hair is white? A group of officers forced her to shower, and when she came out of the bathroom, I didn't recognize her. She was mad as a white-headed wet hen, though. That meant she'd have to start from scratch on the hair and makeup. That type of maintenance can't be easy!

Joyce's voice reminds me of Aunt Bea of Mayberry—there's a singsong quality to it. And she's even built a lot like Aunt Bea—short but not quite as round. Aunt Bea was nice. Joyce is a sneaky, argumentative know-it-all.

Remember the movie *Whatever Happened to Baby Jane?* If someone makes the movie of Joyce's life, Bette Davis will surely be cast as the lead. Even if Bette's dead, she could still play the role.

Wednesday, September 30, 1987

Dear Nancy,

My bad handwriting is even worse than usual because my hands are still partially numb from spending the day squeezed in handcuffs, but I want to tell you this tale while it's still fresh in my mind.

I spent most of the day at Livingston County Courthouse with a group of my rowdy friends. Remember our problem with frisky male guards who are frisk-happy? Well, we prisoners filed a class action suit in federal court—and today we attended a hearing.

Federal Judge Joseph "Little Joe" Stephens appointed to us a very kind, gentle, and cute Kansas City attorney named Paul Shy. They both are World War II-generation men who respect women— even bad girls like us.

Six of my trouble-making compadres and I received tickets to the show and were decked out in prison jewelry to attend. Shackles and chains. The heavy metal look.

First of all, we inmates testified individually. I'm no fan of witness stands, but since my life didn't depend on the outcome of this hearing, I felt as relaxed as a person can feel in handcuffs and leg shackles.

Stories of male guards, who fondle us in the name of security, were told. Judge Stephens listened sympathetically to every word, bless his heart. Some also told of years of physical bullying at the hands of men—husbands, boyfriends, and even blood kin. Relaying these memories brought the onset of tears. Lots of emotion. It's difficult to hear and feel the pain from victims of sexual and physical abuse.

We also explained that the searches were mostly targeted to finding cookies. Yes. Cookies. Cookies that were served to us on our trays at chow. Cookies that guards feared we might sneak back to our cells to nibble or dunk in coffee. And yes, the canteen sells cookies, so cookies outside the chow hall are not an issue.

Then the assistant superintendent (warden) testified. She's a big-busted Black lady who kept running her hands all over her own breasts to emphasize the subject at hand. It was embarrassing. At one point, while digging in her ample cleavage, she called a woman's bosom "The Bank of America" where valuables are hidden. We leaned back in our seats in horror.

The greasy guard who started all this uproar took the stand wearing his Sunday best: high-water brown polyester officer uniform trousers with a white way-too-tight, short-sleeved cowboy shirt stretched over his beer belly. Judge Stephens glared down at him while he stuttered and stumbled through his explanation as to why he must thoroughly search our breasts, buttocks, and inner thighs to keep America safe.

It occurred to me that his wife might be sitting in the gallery, so I scanned the room to catch a glimpse of an irate spouse. I spied several. In fact, the courtroom was crowded. Looked like the whole town turned out.

Then the major, the head of custody, took the stand. He freely admitted that he ran the prison just fine before August 1986—when the law changed. He didn't need male guards to grope the prisoners in the name of security. He also agreed that cookies are the reason for the after-chow pat searches. The sour superintendent shot sharp poison darts at him with her dark eyes, but he didn't appear to notice.

All in all, we feel that the hearing went well. Of course, we must wait for the judge to ponder and hand down his decision. We're praying he sees the violation of our human rights and puts a stop to the guards' license to feel us up at will.

We seven are keeping watchful eyes on the staff here who have taken umbrage to this suit. Don't worry, we watch each other's backs.

January 15, 1988

Dearest Momma, Daddy, and Kids,

You'll never guess who came to see me today. Not to the visiting room—to my actual ROOM—my cell! While all bundled up because the room is freezing and perched on my bunk crocheting furiously on that big navy bedspread I'm making for Sarah, I saw the top of the superintendent's head pass by the little window of my door.

The superintendent never comes in the housing unit. Never. So, I was preparing to jump down off the bunk and investigate when keys opened my door and two strange women came in. The superintendent and a sergeant stood in the doorway guarding them. I conducted the whole visit still sitting on my bunk looking down at my company. There's not enough room for three people on the floor of my cell.

It turned out that one of the ladies is Democratic State Representative Sue Shear, from St. Louis. The other lady works for an alternative-to-prison sentencing organization.

I suppose I should back up and explain that I wrote every legislator in the state a few months ago. I designed a letter explaining our plight, and with Momma's help on the postage, every member of the General Assembly was contacted. There are around 160 of them!

Rep. Sue Shear actually came to see me. She's very nice, articulate, extremely intelligent, and told me that she just had to meet me. She wants to help women who have been sentenced to no-parole sentences. According to her, women receive the sentence much more commonly than men. So, I'm going to be her "inside" contact person. THIS IS SO EXCITING!

Can't wait to tell Mrs. Kline, the Platt Junior College instructor for whom I clerk/tutor. Remember you met her at graduation? Mrs. Kline is a rose among thorns—and a great instructor. She takes special interest in all her students. Even helps them find employment when they parole. Clerking for her is a joy because of her positive attitude and loving nature.

When I was writing those letters, addressing the envelopes, licking stamps to place on each, and sticking them in the mail slot, I felt as if I was placing messages in bottles and throwing them out into the sea—hoping and praying that someone will find at least one and rescue me from this island of confinement.

Anyway, Rep. Shear found the bottle marked with her name, read the message, and wants to throw us a life jacket.

April 18, 1988

Dear Mary,

I love fried eggs...over easy...the whites solid but the yellows runny. Yum. Since I keep a watchful eye on the posted breakfast menu, I never miss Fried Egg Day. This morning was Fried Egg Day.

While sitting all alone in the dining room savoring my toast and eggs, which were hot and as perfect as prison eggs can get, I was witness to a couple of early morning grouches.

Yes, in prison I have discovered the hard way that most women fail to rise out of bed bright-eyed and bushy tailed. I've learned to keep a lid on my natural crack-of-dawn cheerfulness. Inmates have less tolerance for "chipper" before noon.

Anyway, the problem was between two inmates: one tiny dark-haired white girl behind the line serving and one large Black handkerchief-headed potential breakfast-eater. The large gal said something negative to the tiny girl. I didn't overhear—just caught the quick reaction.

Before the big one even finished her comments, the little one flew up over the serving line as if she had a small trampoline hidden behind the counter. Perfect arch. The move was amazing and beautiful. Any gymnastic teacher would have been proud.

The perfect leap ended in a frontal tackle. She grabbed the big one by the neck. The combination of surprise and speed gave the little one the advantage and the power to topple the big one over backwards.

Both fell with a loud thud on the floor in front of me, the little one on top. The thump was the sound of the big girl's head bouncing on the concrete floor. (That had to hurt.)

Obviously, this was not the girl's first rodeo. Wonder if she's ever taken an anger management class. Don't think I'll suggest it to her, though.

While keeping an eye on the activity, I moved my breakfast tray and plastic glass of milk back to a safer table. My eggs were still hot, and I wasn't about to stop eating just because the "floor show" had moved dangerously close to my feet.

I've turned into such a good little inmate. Never missed a beat. Consumed a good hot breakfast while two people tried to kill each other.

As I took my last bite, the guard arrived and pulled the little girl off. Show's over. Perfect timing. As my former cellie Theresa always reminded me, "It's all just live entertainment."

Later the guard asked me for a witness statement, but I couldn't be of any help. "See, sir, I love fried eggs. I was so busy eating that I didn't see a doggone thing. Sorry. I do love fried eggs, and mine were nearly perfect."

September 20, 1988

Dearest Kids,

Remember Cheri, my red-headed little friend who's Jane's exact age? Did I tell you that she saw the parole board and received an excellent parole date? She will serve 8 1/3 years, which is really good.

While planning for her big hearing, we decided she needed to look as young and innocent as possible, so I lucked upon a few yards of a dainty, blue-flowered lightweight cotton in the donated odds and ends at Recreation. You know I can sew anything, so I made a dress pattern out of newspapers just like Granny Snow taught me and hand sewed a simple drop-waist summer dress for her. She looked like a DOLL in it.

I made a similar dress out of red handkerchief print for Eve, my friend from Hungary. She has so little, and when I gave the plain cotton dress to her, she cried.

Eve's husband brought her back to the U.S. when he was in the service but abused her terribly. The tension mounted until a fight ended with him dead. She's serving a fifteen-year sentence, but her husband's mother attends every parole board hearing and screams vengefully to block her parole. The former mother-in-law evidently refuses to see that her son was no saint.

My tiny Hungarian pal is into body building and quite good at it. Channeling a lifetime of pain and frustration into this endeavor is beneficial. She swore she would coach me into building muscles, too, but my scrawny limbs stubbornly remain scrawny no matter what. I do love aerobics, though. It's like dancing and therefore fun.

Poor Eve has been in GED class for years. She's so frustrated and feels stupid, but I told her that I'd never ever pass a GED test in Hungary! Would you?

Another friend is a gypsy. A real one. She can't read a word and tells me that female gypsies are not permitted to learn to read. Isn't that amazing? I tutor her, which is not easy. I don't suggest people wait until they are in their fifties to start reading. Oh, but she can read palms—preferably palms crossed with silver.

On the other end of the education spectrum is Lucy, my roommate. She earned a degree in biochemistry from the University of Missouri and was a pre-vet student. Wonder how she landed in here?

Lucy fell in love with an easygoing, tall handsome man who became a cop. The career move was not good for his soul. He began using the drugs he confiscated from suspects and became mean. Shortly after Lucy gave birth to their son, postpartum depression and the spousal abuse and battering caused her to try to put an end to it all. Her husband was also in the middle of another tirade. I think both factors were at fault.

However it began, while wrestling for his service revolver, the gun accidentally fired. He was dead; Lucy was hysterical. She called the police, her husband's friends, who promptly rearranged the crime scene to make it appear that Lucy had shot her sleeping, bedded husband.

The jurors realized that the blood spatters and other pathological evidence didn't jive, but there was that dead body for which to account—so they compromised and handed her twelve years for second-degree murder.

Since she's been in prison, her former mother-in-law has worked tirelessly to gain total custody of her son so that Lucy can never see him again. The good, upstanding, well-to-do mother of the drug addict cop seems to look much better to the court than the hapless inmate mother of the little boy.

Lucy's pain breaks my heart. She loved her husband so much. Still does. She loves her son with every fiber of her being. He was only an infant when she was taken away from him. Occasionally the two of them are permitted to visit, but even though she writes him all the time and sends gifts, he really doesn't know her. Lucy's a fragile soul, and I fear she will never find peace or happiness in her life again. Hope I'm wrong.

I can't imagine never seeing your kids again. I count my blessings every day, because I have had the opportunity to retain my status as your mother. And am able to watch you all grow up—even if from afar.

December 20, 1988

Dearest Sade, Matt, Carrie, and Bunky,

The other night during what they call Advanced Art class, our college instructor asked where Peggy was. The teacher remembered her from our prior course.

Peggy is memorable because she's such a total biker chick. She wears only clothes with the Harley motorcycle logo on it. Where does she find this stuff? Anyway, she even crocheted an afghan with the Harley logo emblazoned across the yarn—for her "ol' man." That's how she refers to her husband: "my ol' man."

She should be in a movie! Peggy sports strawberry-blonde hair—cut short in the front and on top and way long in the back—and a sweet pale freckled-face lit with blue eyes. If we wrestled her into a nice, long-sleeved dress and dainty heels, and we'd have to, she'd blend into a PTA meeting. But oh, no, Peggy wouldn't be caught dead in regular clothes. Her black boots are big-soled heavy for riding motorcycles. Her jeans are skintight, worn, and ride low on her narrow hips. Harley tattoos adorn her slender arms and legs.

In answer to this question, I spoke up, "Oh, Peggy is too short to take this class."

The teacher, who's a tall woman—even taller than me—pulled

herself up to her full height, indignantly thrust her hands onto her hips and loudly queried the entire group. "What do you mean she's too short to take the class? We would never discriminate against anyone because of physicality!"

We all laughed. You see, Peggy just happens to stand less than five feet, but that had nothing to do with my explanation. In prison lingo, if a person is scheduled to leave prison soon, she's described as "short"—as in, she has a short time left to serve. Peggy is supposed to leave here in a week or two, which means she doesn't have time to complete the course.

After we explained the prison meaning of "short" to our teacher, we told her about "short and shitty." When someone is near the end of her prison time, she invariably becomes antsy—as you can imagine. Kinda like that feeling near the end of the school year when the sunshine is luring you outside—and you feel like you'll burst if vacation doesn't come soon. In here that craziness is known as "short and shitty."

I'll use the phrase in a prison sentence: "Peggy is fin 'ta parole in twelve days and a wake-up, so I won't bother her with all that. She's getting really short 'n shitty, ya know."

September 15, 1989

Dear Nancy,

Representative Sue Shear has arranged for a special legislative hearing to be held here at the prison. Nothing like this has ever been attempted.

About a dozen of us who are serving no-parole sentences will testify. Speechwriting is not these people's forte—much less speech giving! And this subject is very emotional. My friend Helen and I are working with each lady to write her speech—one that includes her story—or a portion of it. Pulling hen's teeth would be easier.

Few like to think about that part of their past, much less talk about it. I've privately interviewed a couple of them so far and pieced together their tales of woe so that I can try to write up a talk for them that they can actually give.

Haven't even written mine yet but have decided to just go for it straightforwardly—from the murder to today. The fact that all the evidence was not available at trial is a big point for people who think that trials are the end result of a panel of knowledgeable jurists. I could talk for days but will cut it down to about fifteen minutes.

This show is scheduled for next month, and I have a lot of work to do, so I'll close, Nancy. Wish us luck in our quest to enlighten lawmakers as to the hopelessness and injustice of no-parole sentences!

October 18, 1989

Testimony from Special Legislative Hearing
Chillicothe Correctional Center

My story is long and complicated, so I have decided to leave out the prosecutor's opinions and conjectures and stick only with what has happened. Some of you have heard or read bits and pieces but don't have a clear picture of the events. I sincerely hope the following gives you some insight into what occurred and what my family has gone through during the past five and a half years.

In the early morning hours of February 18, 1984, I was awakened by what I thought was a clap of thunder. Before I knew what happened, I was yanked out of bed by the hair, thrown on the floor, and pinned down by a man who held a knife to my throat with one hand and removed my pajama bottoms and panties with the other. All I can remember that he said was, "I hate it when they cry." But I couldn't stop crying.

When he got off me and left the room, I climbed over the bed to my husband. He had been shot but was making weak, ragged breathing noises. I pulled on my clothes, tried the phone by the bed, which was dead, and ran to the other bedrooms to check our children, who, thank God, were all sleeping and unharmed.

I knew that my husband needed medical attention, so I woke

the kids and told them that we had a small fire and had to leave the house. When we reached the bottom of the stairs, as I was pulling coats on the small boys, twelve-year-old Sarah slipped into the living room to retrieve her beloved flute. Eight-year-old Carrie went, too. They both saw a flashlight under the basement door but assumed it was their father.

We drove to a neighbor's house a couple of miles away. It's amazing that Cliff understood my gibberish, but he did and raced to town for help. The kids and I huddled on the couch in their living room until the ambulance stopped in front of the house. The neighbor lady and I went outside where the ambulance driver told us that Bill was dead. With weak knees I made my way back to tell our children. That was just the beginning of our nightmare that won't end.

My five children and I were in shock, but when asked to come to the police station for questioning, of course we went. We thought it was important to help the authorities. Even after I was questioned about Bill's life insurance policies (we had recently dropped a large policy on him and taken out a large policy on me, but that didn't seem to have any bearing) and asked to take a nitrate test to determine if I had fired a firearm recently, I was too stupid to see that they thought I had killed my husband. Of course I consented to take the nitrate test there and then because I had nothing to hide. The test confirmed that I had not fired a gun.

Two days after the murder, I was again questioned by the police for more than seventeen hours straight. At this time they made it quite clear that I was THE suspect—the ONLY suspect. During that night I was taken to the highway patrol and given a "lie detector" test but have never been told the results. I assume the results were in my favor since the investigators never harassed me about it.

After that test, while waiting beside the police car, I shivered since I was without a coat in the cold winter air and anemic to boot. One of the investigators asked why I was shaking so I explained, "I'm cold-blooded and get chilly easily." Later during the trial, that police investigator quoted what I said out of context and made it seem that I had meant cold-blooded killer. That's the kind of police who worked on this case. They did not allow me to attend the family night services for my husband and did not return me to my worried friends until early morning.

The next day at the funeral, police were everywhere watching us and who we talked to. It would have been horrible enough if Bill had died in an accident, but this was almost unbearable.

A couple of days later, the sheriff came to our friends' farm where we were staying and arrested me in front of my children and parents. I was taken to the jail in Warrensburg, fingerprinted, booked, strip searched, and placed in a cell. The female officer who searched me commented on the horrible bruises on my body. Within a few hours I was released to an attorney whom my parents had called in.

The kids and I desperately needed an income, so we decided we had to reopen the family lumber company. That was a very difficult decision since that business had been so important to Bill and everything there reminded us of him. But we did reopen, and the community supported us. I was even given a high school girls' softball team to coach that summer.

I did not go to trial until April of the next year—1985. During that time I slept little—always listening for an intruder in the night. We had many prowlers and called our poor neighbors many times for help. We were even robbed once, but when the police came, they were absolutely no help. They refused to take fingerprints or even check out the man-sized footprints in the snow, which led from the front door to the road. The same police officers, who had told me that no one could have forced entry into our home when my husband was killed, told me that "anyone could have gotten in anyway."

The neighbors gave us an English setter who was a fantastic watchdog. The kids and I were so relieved to have him in the house with us. I could hear him walk from bed to bed at night checking on his family. One day when we came home, we found him dead in the yard—poisoned. By then we were not only terrified, we were extremely frustrated.

My attorney advised a change of venue, so after much debate with the prosecutor, the trial was held in Sedalia. Each morning I was offered another plea bargain better than the last. I stubbornly refused each one. I truly believed that since I was not guilty, I would not be convicted. I was tragically wrong.

My trial took four long days. Three of my children testified on my behalf, and I can still envision their scared little faces as they sat on the stand. Seven-year-old Morgan wrote notes saying things like, "We don't like you," or "You're bad guys," folded them into paper airplanes, and sailed them to the police who looked on, sheepishly. At each recess the kids would run into the courtroom and huddle around me until it was time to start again.

When we were called in for the verdict, as soon as I saw the first juror's face, I knew that all was lost. Not one could even look at me. When the juror pronounced, "Guilty," my children screamed, ran out of the courtroom, down the stairs, and into the street. No one who was there will ever forget that horrendous moment.

I was released the next day on an appeal bond and went home to my children. I soon heard from a neighbor who had read the account of the trial in the local newspaper. She had seen a white sedan with one occupant parked near her home the night of Bill's murder. The man was parked in a spot where our house would have been clearly visible. She'd told the sheriff about it the day of the murder and thought he would have told my attorney, but he didn't.

My attorney, upon hearing of this new evidence, went back to court with it, but the judge decided that evidence of an unknown man in the vicinity of the murder would NOT have made a difference in my trial. Not long after that hearing, I was summoned back to court because the prosecutor didn't appreciate the fact that I was home and not in prison. The court raised my appeal bond to a $250,000 cash bond. I spent a few days in jail before my dear family raised the bond amount.

That summer we once again reopened the lumberyard in order to have an income. I enrolled at the University of Central Missouri in Warrensburg. I decided that if I were cleared, we needed a way to make a living, and I've always wanted to be a teacher. I also wanted to be a good example for my children and make them familiar with a college campus.

I had our business open in the mornings, and I attended classes in the afternoons. All the while the kids and I knew that any day I might be picked up by the police. We never knew which day the appellate court might deny my appeal and I'd be taken to prison. Our close family became even closer, and every parting was treated as if it might be our last.

In April 1986, we received a call informing us that my appeal had been denied. We packed up and drove to my parents' house. I wanted to make sure that the children would not be separated and put into foster care. We spent the rest of the weekend saying goodbye. On Monday morning my parents drove me to the authorities, and I turned myself in.

In the summer of 1986, just a few months after I was incarcerated, my friends and family compiled and submitted a petition of many signatures from our community to the governor asking for a pardon. It was referred to the Parole Board and promptly denied without any investigation.

Meanwhile I am working my way through the slow, complicated, and horribly expensive appeal process. I had a public defender for a time, but he was practically worthless. He rarely answered my letters and never spoke to me before the hearing last November. Out of frustration my parents retained another lawyer and have spent $15,000 since May. I HATE that they are pouring their life savings into this legal rat hole.

My dear mother writes me every day and keeps me well informed about my kids. We have an amazingly strong and loving family, and they are very protective of my children who have been hurt so much. People can be so cruel—especially to a child who has a parent in prison.

The people who care about me are having difficulty understanding my sentence. Every once in a while, I get a letter from an old friend who says something like, "Maybe you'll be home for this Christmas if you get off for good behavior." These are adults, and they can't seem to understand that I will NEVER come home under this sentence. Can you imagine how my children must feel?

November 4, 1989

Dear Nancy,

Well, we pulled it off. The special legislative hearing went very well, I think. At least we all spoke, and no one fainted.

The ladies did a good job. Everyone cried. We can't talk about such traumas with no emotion, but I think we got the point across through the veil of tears.

One of the women spoke about the change in laws. For example, Kathy killed her husband in June 1977 and received a life sentence with parole, which was the law at the time. In October of the same year, Carlene was involved in the murder of her husband and because the sentencing law changed in August, she's serving life with no parole for fifty years. Same degree of murder charge—different time.

Kathy will leave after twelve years of confinement. Carlene will not see the parole board for the first consideration hearing until she's served fifty years—twelve versus fifty. Big gap.

Helen told us about years of emotional and physical abuse administered by her late husband and how evidence of this torture could not be used as a legal defense in court in Missouri. Battered woman syndrome, it's called.

Another spoke about how the very same crime can receive from 120 days to five years to ten years to fifteen to twenty-five to life with no parole depending on the county where it originated, the prosecutor, and the political climate. Plea agreements make a big difference, too. If you take the deal, you're much better off than if you don't. That's why we've noticed that the guilty, who have criminal backgrounds and know the system, do much less time than the naively innocent.

Our sweet "pat search" attorney Paul Shy drove all the way from Kansas City to attend. My Platt Junior College business teacher Mrs. Kline was there, too. Some Department of Corrections bigwigs came because they hate no-parole sentences. Prisoners who have no hope are more difficult to control—where's the incentive?

An Irish priest, who the old-timer girls obviously love, drove from Jeff City. Father Behan gathered us all in the teacher's lounge to hold hands and share a group prayer before the show.

Rep. Dale Whiteside from Chillicothe sat on the panel. Recently I'd met him at a GED graduation when he was a guest speaker. Senator Larry Rohrbach from California, Missouri, parked next to him. Of course, the feisty little Sue Shear ran the show.

I'll enclose a copy of my speech and would enclose copies of the others, but I have none.

Rumor has it that we bad girls are to be transferred back to Renz near Jeff City. We're just sick about it. The big Platt Junior College boss over Ms. Kline is trying to keep me here, but I doubt he will be able to pull it off. I imagine it's a custody issue, and because of my no-parole sentence, I'm one of the worst security levels.

I'll let you know if the scuttlebutt is true and we are sent back. I really hate this, because this prison is so much closer to my family, and I have a good job here. And Renz is SO dilapidated. Do you remember it? I think you were there only once or twice.

My dear, calm, easy-going Grandpa Snow always advised, "Just let things unravel." He was very Zen in that way. I try hard to follow his wise philosophy and example.

Bunk 'n' Junk

December 16, 1989

Dear Mary,

I'm back at Renz, where I started my prison career. Don't know where to begin. This has been a nightmare inside a nightmare.

At Chillicothe, while guards wound chains around us in preparation for our before-dawn trip, the friends we left behind hugged us and cried farewell. Once we were loaded on the bus, everyone settled in for a silent but tense ride. As the bus neared Jefferson City, nervous chatter began.

Helen sat next to me, wrung her hands as best she could in handcuffs, and fretted. Those of us who had been at Renz before were well aware of how horrid it would be. The newer girls had not a clue—which made their trip easier.

When Helen and I caught sight of the old prison, big tears welled up in her sad eyes. It was true. We were on our way to be redeposited in Hell.

Unloading, unshackling, unchaining, finding our property, sorting through it all with staff, and carrying the boxes up the concrete steps to the top floor was mayhem. I can't begin to describe the disorganization. None of the staff knew what to do or how to do it.

When we finally made our way up to the dorm, and as our

friends, who had arrived two days before, were hugging us in welcome, we looked over their shoulders in disbelief. The windowpanes are cracked—some broken clear out. Ice is frozen on both sides of the remaining glass. The snow blows in. I'm not kidding. Needless to say, it's chilly in here.

Dingy, stain-streaked state sheets have pathetically been stapled to most of the tall windows in a feeble attempt to keep the howling north wind at bay. They blow in and bulge and flap like sails, as if we are lost at sea. Some of the girls say that in the middle of the night, the sheets look to them like gray ghosts straining to enter—and the eerie moan of the wind only adds to the illusion.

But the cold is not the worst part. The filth is. Nicotine is so thick on the walls that the cracked concrete looks like it was painted with thick brushfuls of walnut stain—and the stain ran. The small, rusted metal tables provided for each cubicle are covered on one side or the other with a thick stubborn layer of crud made out of dust, straw, cobwebs, and manure that formed when the furniture was stacked and stored in the barn—since the War Between the States, I think. The hollow, rusted-iron bunk bed posts are completely full of cigarette butts. I refuse to describe the showers and toilets since you might be eating supper while reading this. Men, nasty men, have had this prison for three years, and it shows.

The odor. Lord, the strong odor of men's urine and stale sweat plus old tobacco plus other indescribable stench permeates the air. How can it stink so badly with so much ventilation? One of the girls keeps a bandana tied around her nose like an old-time bank robber. In defense, she rubbed the scarf with a magazine perfume sample. Good idea.

Our chairs are upside-down, empty, plastic pickle buckets. As I sit and scribble this, a permanent and perfect circle is embedding itself in my butt.

And I didn't even see the mess in all its glory. The first wave of women had been cleaning for two days before we arrived. Unbelievable.

Because there are still male inmates housed in this camp, we're on lockdown status—and don't know how long that will be. Platt

Junior College has a paralegal class here and offered me a job, so I'll be back at work soon.

At CCC we lived in cells for the most part: two or four-woman rooms. But Renz Farm's housing is open bays. Rows of rusted iron bunk beds in big open rooms. No privacy. Burning up in the summer; frigid in the winter. At least with the cold, the roaches aren't so troublesome.

I've never seen my compadres look so worn. They're sporting dark circles under their haunted eyes from the strain. We resemble raccoons who suffer from severe insomnia. No one is sleeping well. We're cold, crowded, and crazed.

Many of the guards have never worked with females and don't seem to want to. They are mean and rude—can't understand why we demand mops and cleaning supplies. Some of the old guards remember and have warmly welcomed us. They look forward to a cleaner, sweeter smelling, "kinder, gentler" work environment.

My theory is that the-powers-that-be want the legislature to appropriate funds to build a new women's prison, and we're pawns in the plan. If we holler about the abhorrent conditions, maybe they'll get the money.

Meanwhile, we will clean this place up and try to make the best of a bad situation. That's what we do best.

February 19, 1990

Dear Nancy,

This morning on my way to work, I carried a Black's Law Dictionary. A young, serious, military-looking guard stopped me with, "What's that?"

"A book," I pronounced carefully in case he'd never heard of one.

"You can't take an entertainment device to your job detail."

There is indeed a rule on the books preventing us from taking novels and Walkmans to certain job details, although many supervisors don't have a problem with workers who get the job done and want to read quietly. But I work in the Education Department where books are not only welcome, they are required.

"Well, sir, I work at the school—next to the library—where the books are kept...."

"I don't care. No entertainment devices at a job detail."

With a dismissing flip of my insolent hand, I explained as I resumed my walk to work, "Don't worry. This book isn't that entertaining."

June 12, 1990

Dear Nancy,

If you wonder where I've been, the Mighty Missouri flooded again, and we had to evacuate. "Bunk and junk" is the prison term for packing up and getting out. Renz is right next to the river! The old-timers tell me we will bug out all through the flood season.

After we packed up our pillowcases with as many necessities as we could, we were quickly shackled, chained, and loaded into prison buses. We "high-security levels" were escorted to the men's diagnostic prison at Fulton about thirty miles away, I believe. The "low-security" among us were bused to the Church Farm prison on the other side of the river—the high side.

My bad-girl compadres and I camped on the gym floor for days—I'm not really sure how long. When you're locked up in a big room with nothing to do, keeping track of time is not an issue. We only left the gym for meals and showers—except for now and then when the group was allowed out into a dog pen for some much-needed fresh air.

Unfortunately, the trip back here was torture, for me. The transportation guards ran out of handcuffs, so they used narrow plastic strapping on us. The plastic is the kind that's wrapped around electrical supplies—or around boxes. It's tough stuff—the Incredible Hulk couldn't break it with his bare hands. It must be cut off.

Anyway, because my hands and wrists are so small—one of my

53

friends says I have pygmy paws—the stranger-guard pulled the binding very tight, so I could not slip my hands out. But what if I did? I would still fly down the highway locked in a prison bus followed by armed guards led by Highway Patrol no matter where my hands were. They've watched too many movies.

While on the bus jostling down the highway, the unforgiving band cut into my skin over the wrist bone. By the time we arrived back at Renz, my hands and clothes were red with my blood. I felt as if I might pass out from the pain and tried my best to push to the head of the band-snipping line to get the bloody band cut off. But I was not the only one in trouble.

I'm loathe to admit it, but I actually bawled like a big baby while waiting my turn. Why would they use something like that?

Many of the others pointed out the devastation and debris left by the flood—a mess we would soon clean up, but I could only think about my wounded wrists. When the band was finally severed, I carefully pulled it free from the gash it had cut. What a relief!

Recently I had breast surgery. Nothing serious. I found a lump, so I was transported to Calloway County Hospital to have it removed and biopsied. I'm fine now, but I used some of the salve, gauze, and tape from that experience to tidy up my hurt wrist—and it's healing very nicely already.

Oh, Major Turner retired, so we have a brand-new superintendent, Bryan Goeke. He sure took over at a great time. Nothing like flood, famine, and pestilence to start your reign.

July 29, 1990

Dear Nancy,

Residents Encounter Christ, REC, is a great, multidenominational Christian organization that conducts three-day retreat-like programs with prisons in Missouri and Illinois. The weekends are awesome. A vacation from incarceration. I know I've mentioned them to you before.

We're planning another weekend and always hold a meeting with team members, both inmates and free volunteers, to organize. We call ourselves "inside and outside" teams.

At this last meeting, as an ice breaker, we were asked to quote a favorite Bible verse when we introduced ourselves to the group. This meeting was held in the college classroom where I clerk in the afternoons. The room is decorated with short motivational sayings that I found and printed out on Apple IIe software called Printshop.

When it was Father Behan's turn to give a Bible verse, with a twinkle in his Irish eye, he quoted one of my posters instead, "Blessed are the flexible for they shall not be bent out of shape."

You should have seen the poker faces of these good people. They all tried their best to not look stumped. They actually thought he was serious. After all, he is a priest. Priests aren't practical jokers, are they?

One sweet little white-haired lady in the back of the room discreetly flipped through her King James, searching. No one said a word about his choice.

You probably wonder how I ever started attending Catholic Mass. Well, this little Protestant tried and tried to find a prison church service that fit. Some of these religious groups bring in huge, tall speakers, crank them up, and scream to the Lord as if He were deaf. Scary!

And the rolling around on the chapel floor speaking gibberish is not for me either—although if that's your cup of tea, go for it. During the first service I attended, when everyone but me seemed to be gripped by a group seizure, I ran! I got out of that place as fast as I could. Ms. J, the recreation officer who was supervising that particular service, couldn't quit laughing. She told me that my eyes were big as saucers as I fled.

When we came back to Renz in December, Father Behan kept sending invitations to me to come to Mass. We met last year at the special legislative hearing Rep. Sue Shear sponsored at Chillicothe. I kept sending back messages, "Thanks, but I'm not Catholic."

But he's a persistent man, so I gave in and promised I'd come to one service. Just one. But that night I found my spiritual home. Not only do we quietly worship with no mega sound system, he teaches us. Every Friday night we learn pieces of biblical history and theory. ("When the student is ready, the teacher will appear.") It's fascinating. And we have fun, too. He's not stuffy—he's Irish, and kinda reminds me of my mother: honest to a fault AND full of blarney.

Everyone is welcome. He patiently explains the rituals—the why and how they came to be. Father says, "All roads lead to the one God." With open arms, he embraces all people from all cultures and beliefs. I like that. He's seen too much prejudice and conflict in his native land. He can hardly tolerate bigotry and meanness. I think if the earthbound Jesus had been Irish, he would have been a lot like Father B.

April 24, 1991

Dear Mary,

Have I ever told you about PATCH (Parents and Their Children)? It's an organization involving volunteers from the community, staff, inmates, and their families. The goal is to bring incarcerated mothers and their children closer together by providing home-like visits in a house trailer. I'm on the PATCH board and do all I can to raise funds and help wherever needed.

Many kids would never get to visit their moms if it weren't for PATCH. Some families have no transportation available or can't afford the trip. I'm one of the lucky ones because my family goes out of their way to visit me.

My kids adore PATCH visits because we're not under scrutiny by the guards and are allowed to cuddle and even roll on the floor like normal people in a normal family for a few hours. The best reason is because I can cook for them. Fried potatoes are their favorite dish, and we laboriously peel and slice the tubers with plastic knives.

PATCH operates on donations and fundraisers. June, the PATCH lady, takes her "dog and pony show" to churches and solicits donations. In here we also sponsor walkathons and BBQs.

The PATCH Walkathon is a huge annual event, usually held in the fall when it's not too hot. Inmates collect pledges for the miles they will walk around the quarter-mile track—anywhere from one cent to one dollar a mile usually. PATCH provides beverages and snacks for everyone who turns out to walk, visit, have fun, and collect money for our kids.

Father Behan is the biggest duck in the puddle. He not only pledges a big amount, he also walks with us—not a little either. He sometimes does fifteen miles!

The summer PATCH BBQ is great. Even our superintendent helps cook. We charge the inmates, staff, and visitors for plates of good food and hope to make a profit.

The PATCH Christmas party is a special evening. We serve all sorts of pie—REAL pie donated by sweet little free ladies. Doc Kayser, a local chiropractor, dresses up like Santa, hugs all the residents and staff, and gives his gift bags of hygiene items. We sing and laugh and have quite a celebration. If it wasn't for PATCH, Christmas would be pretty dismal.

Helen and I took pie to the new girls who are confined in R&O. (Receiving and Orientation is the area where new inmates are held while educated in the rules and cleared medically. It's the sad purgatory of prison. Less freedom than general population.) When we arrived bearing gifts, we found one of the young girls sobbing hysterically into the wall phone to her mother. Our faces dissolved into tears as both Helen and I remembered how we felt when we first arrived. Lost, alone, and terrified.

During Easter weekend, I dress up in a big baggy fake-furry hot-pink rabbit costume and play with the kids in the visiting area giving out candy eggs. That suit is like wearing a huge bathroom rug—HOT. But I love the fact that the little kids buy into the fantasy totally.

They believe I'm the real Easter Bunny and don't realize that I'm just a skinny woman sweating in a fuzzy costume. Even when a bad boy hollered that the Easter Bunny wears Nikes, the small children's faith was not shaken.

The hood of the suit allows my whole face to stick out, so with eyeliner I draw whiskers and a brown nose. I pin and gel my hair back, but loose hairs invariably find their way out and I poke them back with my fake fur mitten-paws. The wire-shaped, satin-lined long ears are always lopsided.

In the past, bad little boys loved to chase me around, snatch off my yarn pom-pom tail, and run away with it. The visiting room officer had to pin it back on over and over. This year I fooled them all and sewed it on securely.

This last Easter while posing with a family for their Easter group shoot, the wheelchair-bound husband grabbed my butt! I was shocked and jerked away. Thinking that either I'd imagined it or that he'd accidently touched me, and being the good sport that I am, I stepped back into the camera frame and smiled. But then he grabbed me again.

Moving my bunny tail around out of easy reach, I whispered in his ear using my meanest tone to offset my comical look, "Grab my ass one more time, bud, and I promise I'll tell your old lady. Right here, right now." His strong, healthy wife sports a no-non-sense attitude—and was right on the other side of his chair.

That jerk must have believed me because he pulled his hands inside the safety of his wheelchair and never even glanced at me again. Don't think he smiled for the picture either.

July 16, 1991

Dear Kids,

This morning while at work, I was called for a surprise visit. Since I'm the Education clerk, I must keep file cabinet keys on me at all times. All the tests and records are locked up for obvious reasons. There are a few thieves in here, you know.

When the phone rang, and the officer on the other line told me that I had a visit, excitedly I locked up, rushed to tell my supervisor, and hurried to the visiting room to find Mary O!

We enjoyed each other's company and chattered like chipmunks until... while standing at the soda pop vending machine, I shoved my thumbs in my pockets and to my horror felt the keys on the fifth pocket of my Levi's. KEYS! I'd forgotten to hang them safely back on their hook in my office.

Those keys open only file cabinets, and one would be hard put to escape to freedom through a file cabinet—but they are KEYS! And at Renz, keys are a big deal.

In shock, I whispered to Mary that I had these blasted keys and how that is not a good thing. We huddled soberly and discussed my options. I could throw them in the trash or flush them and act like I hadn't brought them—that I'd left them on their hook at school. Or I could tell the truth to the guard and throw myself on the mercy of the security staff—but mercy is in short supply around here. What a decision!

I chose the honest way—couldn't just discard the keys and cause problems for my supervisors at school—and a lie never sets right on my soul.

To the guard on duty in the visiting room, I confessed, "Excuse me, ma'am. I inadvertently brought these little ole file cabinet keys with me from school." Nervous smile.

When she saw the four tiny keys in my hand, she reacted just as I had feared. "OH MY GOD! HOW COULD YOU! YOU'RE IN BIG TROUBLE NOW, MISSY!" She grabbed the phone and called for backup.

I envisioned handcuffs snapping on my wrists and a degrading walk to the hole. Mary looked as sick as I felt. In strode the grim sergeant who grilled me. After I sang like a canary about every key I'd ever known, he huffed off and left poor Mary and me alone to stew in the juice of our fear.

The Columbia attorney for whom I clerk part-time appeared and headed straight for me. Jim had never joined me on a visit before. This was all very suspect. The guard on duty thought so, too.

Jim opened his briefcase, spoke loudly to me about grading

papers, then whispered, "Give me the bloody keys." Oh my gosh, he'd been sent by my Education boss to save me from myself, but it was too late.

It was my turn to speak loudly about grading papers, then I leaned in and whispered, "I already gave them to the guard. The sergeant took them about an hour ago."

Jim glared down his nose at me in disgust. He could not complete his rescue mission thanks to stupid me. So, he talked loudly again about grading papers then made a hasty retreat, bless his heart.

Sweet Mary had to leave with no idea what fate awaited me. Her parting hug was so strong that she squeezed the breath right out of me.

But after much debate and countless I'm sorries, it was finally decided that I would slide on this first infraction with NO punishment. "But it had better never happen again." It was such a close shave that I can still feel the razor burn.

Speaking of Jim reminds me of the lecture he gives every new paralegal class. His message will not be lost on you kids—because it contains certain undeniable truths—no matter where you find yourself. He tells the girls:

Prison time can be a complete waste of time, or it can be used to your advantage by working on these three areas: 1) Body, 2) Mind, 3) Spirit.

It's a proven scientific fact that your energy level, self-esteem, stress level, and physical looks are hinged on health. So while you're here, take advantage of the exercise classes, recreation equipment, and team sports. When you build muscle and endurance, you will feel stronger and more peaceful. Also, eat right and stay away from the wham-whams and zoo-zoos sold in canteen. Little Debbie is not your friend. (Wham-whams and zoo-zoos is the prison term for junk food. Little Debbie is the brand of snack cakes sold in our canteen.)

Don't lose your mind in here. Expand it. Take classes. Any classes. Hang out in the library and find books to help you figure out what makes you tick and what makes the world go around. Make it a point to learn something new every single day. Look into methods and means to further your education, because education is the key to economic success.

Most arrive in prison broken-spirited and feeling low. You can remain depressed, frustrated, and angry—or you can do something to raise your spirits. Participate in religious activities. Read spiritual books. Meditate. Pray. Joy is regulated by your spirit. Use this time to heal and grow spiritually.

If nothing else, take the time to fully realize and believe that you are one of God's children and deserve to live a fulfilled and joyful life—no matter what. No matter how you've been used and abused. No matter what you've done to hurt others. No matter what. The lesson of forgiveness for yourself and others is priceless in itself.

As the old convict saying goes, "Do your time. Don't let the time do you."

Improve your physical self, your intellect, and your spirit. The past is just that—past. Use your present to ensure a bright future. Come out on the other side of this experience the better for it. Don't waste your "time."

July 29, 1992

Dear PATCH,

I just want to thank all the people who work together to make the PATCH visits possible.

On July 12 I had my monthly visit. That was the last time I'll ever see my eighteen-year-old son Matthew. He died within the week.

I had a wonderful visit with all five of my children and my two grandsons. At one point, after we had played in the sand around the playground area (we had been doing our Jean-Claude Van Damme imitations trying to perform splits), Matt, three-year-old Zach, and I decided we needed to wash our feet—quickly. The cats must have been using the sand for you know what.

Zach sat on the bathroom counter with his tiny feet in the sink. I stuck my feet in the sink and Zach washed my feet, too. Then

Matt rolled up his jeans legs and eased one of his man-sized feet into the basin. Zach and I both washed Matt's feet. I remember kissing Matt and telling him that it didn't seem very long ago when he was Zach's size.

Later while we were preparing lunch, Matt draped his long lanky frame in a chair at the kitchen table and stole tomatoes out of the salad as fast as Sarah could cut them up. We talked about college and his work. He pointed out the hay scratches on his arms caused by bucking bales. Morgan proudly prodded Matt into showing me his muscles earned by hard ranch work.

After lunch while Jane and I did dishes and talked about babies, Matt and Carrie sat together on the couch and played Trivial Pursuit with June and Sarah. Zach and Morgan played, and Jace napped. I kept stealing glances at Matt and Carrie, who were always so close in age and heart.

Not long before it was time to part, we played Simon Says outside. Matt thought he was too good to get caught, but I finally tricked them all with one brilliant false move. We collapsed on each other with gales of laughter. June soon appeared and took our photos. That's the last picture I will ever have of all five of my children.

On Monday afternoon, July 20, I was called to the PATCH trailer. I found my parents there, and Dad held me while he told me that Matt was dead. There is no other place in the prison suitable for a meeting such as that.

Through the generosity of the staff and PATCH, I was allowed to use the PATCH trailer on Wednesday, July 22, to visit with my remaining four children and grandsons. The PATCH program afforded my little family with a private place to mourn, cry, remember, and just cling to each other. We desperately needed that time and place.

On behalf of my children and parents, I once again just want to thank everyone who works with the program. Few organizations on this earth are as worthwhile.

Halloween, October 31, 1992

Dear Mary,

The girls are remembering Halloweens from the past, and I just told the story of the rainy Halloween when Bunky was almost swept away in the town storm drain.

Out of the cardboard boxes that four one-gallon paint cans come in, we fashioned robot costumes for our five eager trick-or-treaters. These ingenious costumes really turned out cute with the kids' arms sticking out of holes cut out on the sides! Then the robots (pronounced "row-butts" by Matt to everyone's delight) insisted I dress up too, so I donned my old, long pioneer dress and bonnet salvaged from the Lee's Summit centennial celebration years ago. Dressed as a lumberyard owner, Bill drove the getaway pickup truck.

The rain was coming down in sheets when Bill pulled up at Marcia's home. Leaping out of the passenger side and racing to the rear, I opened the camper shell latch and hefted robots down off the tailgate. Morgan, who was known as Bunky in those days, toddled a few feet and promptly fell into the raging water of the deep ditch between the street and Marcia's lawn. The other robots screamed bloody murder as super-momma dove in to save the littlest robot from sweeping with the rest of the rainwater into the boy-sized gaping culvert-hole ahead under the side street.

Somehow, I snagged Bunky and threw him to safety into Marcia's lawn and wrestled this heavily waterlogged pioneer woman out of the water, too. The four hysterical robots ran around by way of the driveway to throw themselves on us. I hugged five saturated cardboard boxes containing my sweet little children to my beating breast. Illuminated by the flash of lightning, the rain pounded with no sign of letting up.

My greedy trick-or-treaters quickly got over this mishap. After all, no one was hurt, so we dripped our way to Marcia's back door. You should have seen her face when she opened the door to see that scary sight. Trick or treat!

After Marcia generously bestowed candy upon us—Matt and

63

the girls still had their bags—and after I refused her gracious offer to take us in and dry us off, I lifted the ruined robots back into the camper shell. When I heaved and sloshed my still heavy, dripping self back into the cab of the pickup, Bill simply put his newspaper down, reached for the gear shift knob while pushing in the clutch with his foot, and without even glancing at me absently asked, "Where to now?"

Mary, you asked about the cartoon smiley sun that I put next to my signature on letters. The bright shining sun is for Matthew, my bright shining son. When Matt died, somehow Zach, in his little-boy mind, got the idea that Matt had turned into the sun. Maybe because the family turns their eyes up to Heaven when speaking of him now. I'm just guessing. But I like the idea. So, I draw a smiling sun on my letters now in memory of our Matthew.

December 25, 1992

Dear Mary,

You will never believe how our Christmas Day began. The whole dorm woke up at seven to the strange scuffing, slapping sound made by an officer using a straw broom to push up the suspended ceiling tiles.

Currently I reside in the honor dorm that is an old building separate from the main white house. It looks like a mechanic shop, a Butler Building—corrugated metal sides and shingles. Inside is a big room full of bunks. The ceiling is what I call "dropped."

A metal strip gridwork has been attached to the walls below the rafters. Four by six light-pressed board rectangles (like bulletin board material) set on top of the metal grid comprising our ceiling. Lots of people use this type of ceiling for a basement remodel.

Once I was forced to move the ceiling tiles when I woke up wet in the middle of a rainstorm because the roof was leaking like a sieve right on me. After I found a few big plastic trash bags, I removed the ceiling tiles above my top bunk and placed the trash bags on the tiles as moisture barriers. That defense worked so well that the leaking rainwater was forced to travel down to the next bunk. I was dry and dozing when I heard Renee holler about the leak over her bed.

Anyway, this pip-squeak had decided that since it's a holiday, we must have hidden hooch in the ceiling. Trust me, no one would keep anything valuable on top of these old flimsy rotten ceiling tiles. All he found was dust and debris. Not only was he noisy, but he was also knocking yucky stuff, like mouse droppings, down on top of everyone.

As you can imagine, this weasel had the chickens in the henhouse clucking then squawking loudly. And to compound his stupidity, he argued. Yes. Before 7:30 on Christmas morning, the emotional holiday that most residents want to sleep or cry away, this guard caused so much hate and discontent that we girls resorted to the mightiest weapon in our arsenal, used only in dire emergencies: Mothers.

Some called their mothers, who in turn called the superintendent, who in turn called the shift supervisor, who in turn came out to the dorm and pulled our troublesome officer outside to read him the riot act. Literally. They told him that the way he was acting would incite a riot. That's the riot act, to me.

When my friends and I returned from church, the kid was standing outside smoking and pouting. Recognizing us as troublemakers, he made a big show of pat searching us—just in case the good church people had slipped us a bottle of Christmas cheer. What a jerk!

In my opinion, guards should undergo some sort of sensitivity training to learn how female felons should be handled! But then how do you impart common sense onto a man like that? Either you have it or you don't. He don't.

Blessed are the Flexible

Tuesday, July 6, 1993

Dear Nancy,

Don't know if you saw the news, but Missouri is experiencing big flooding. And when the Missouri River rises, we at Renz must evacuate.

Jane, Sarah, and Carrie were visiting me on my birthday when a crew of workmen clad in those back-protecting, weight-lifting belt things showed up and dollied all the vending machines out of the visiting room to their truck. That was my first clue that something was happening.

The next morning we hapless inmates bugged out with our pillowcases full of emergency supplies in hand. We are allowed one pillowcase for undies, stingers, clothes, hygiene items, writing supplies, books, and anything else we cannot live without. Like shower shoes. If you don't want to catch prison rot, you must wear plastic thong sandals. They are absolutely essential. (A stinger is a small electrical appliance that consists of an electrical cord with a pronged plug-in on one end and a metal heating element on the other. Put the heating coil in a cup of water, then plug the thing in. The coil gets hot as can be and in no time, you have boiling water. We make coffee water with them and can also boil a ramen soup.

I've seen girls make macaroni and cheese with a stinger. Stingers are invaluable tools in prison, but don't ever touch the hot coil.)

My compadres and I are now camping in the gym at Church Farm, a men's prison on the high side of the river. There are around 200 army cots rowed up in this old gym. That's a whole lot of women trapped in one area.

The day before yesterday we were actually allowed to venture outside and get some much-needed fresh air. A group of us were walking around the shady front yard when we heard, "HEY! RED!"

We turned our heads simultaneously and looked at the biggest bare-chested man I ever saw. His hair was long and blonde, and he sported an upside-down handlebar moustache thing, and he was bench pressing a huge truck axle with the wheels attached... it seemed.

I'm serious. This giant's arms are bigger than the two of us combined! He threw down the weight which bounced and clanged, lunged at the chain-link fence almost breaking through, and hollered again even more forcefully, "HEY! RED!"

Betty's shaky voice sounded like a frightened little girl when she whispered, "Patty, he's looking at YOU!" ME? OH, MY, GOSH! I was wearing a red tank top with blue shorts. He was directing his attention to ME!

The largest and scariest man in the universe then started yelling explicit deviant activities to which he thought I should be introduced. Nancy, I didn't even understand most of it—but I KNEW they would not be good for little ole me.

My friends and I were absolutely rooted to the ground. Then when our legs could move, we scurried off like the Our Gang kids stumbling over each other. It was exactly like those old-time movies, "Feets don't fail me now."

We ran to our guard like scared chicks to their momma hen. He looked sick, like he wished we'd gone the other way. As a little Barney Fife-type guy, he knows his limitations.

The wrestler-looking guy kept screaming, so our guard decided quickly that it would be best for us to retire for the day. No argument from any of us chickens. We practically ran Barney over in our haste to retreat into the safety of our hot henhouse.

Yesterday, we were allowed to go back out to the same yard. What the heck. We decided to give it another try. Fresh air is all we want—you can't imagine how stinky it is in the crowded gym. It stunk of old gym socks and men when we arrived, but 200 women sweating in the 100-degree room have not helped the aroma.

So, we followed our guard out—right behind. "We're behind you 100 percent." No one was in the fenced-off weight area, thank Heaven. Our little group relaxed and walked and talked and enjoyed the hot summer day.

The prison is in the country and a small herd of cattle grazed on the other side of the fence. They were a source of amazement to the city girls. That's the closest most of them have ever been to a cow. Made me homesick.

Out of the blue we heard, "HEY! YELLA!" Oh, no, I was wearing a yellow tank top!

The giant was back. Nancy, it was terrifying. If he got his monster hands on me, he could snap me like a dry twig. I've never seen anyone so BIG and CRAZED! And again he hollered really rude and crude suggestions about what he'd like to do to me.

I wasn't the only one with her hair standing on end. Every woman out there looked horrified as we watched him leap up on the fence and rattle the chain violently just like a gorilla in the zoo—except gorillas don't hurl threats in English to the observers. Mommas would never take their kids to the zoo again if they did!

Just as I was about to repeat my actions from the day before and run for the relative protection of the skinny guard, four burley Church Farm guards (handlers) emerged from a side door, pried and pulled the blonde primate off the fence, and dragged him kicking and screaming back into the ape house.

We had been saved! Hallelujah! No one breathed a bigger sigh of relief than Barney. I was a close second, though.

Wednesday, July 14, 1993

Dear Janie, Loran, Zach, and Jace,

We're still on summer vacation at Church Farm. Michelle and I
have decided to make the best of the experience. This prison canteen sells canned salmon and canned peaches—two foods we hav-
en't seen in years. We are making pigs of ourselves. And, no, we
don't mix the two. And their chow-hall food is much better than
ours. These men are good cooks! Since there is no place to exercise, I may put on some weight. Eat, sleep, and growl.

The stage on the side of the gym houses a big TV. Bill, the Recreation guy, asked us for video rental suggestions, so I asked for
The Man from Snowy River. On the last birthday I celebrated in
the free world with Matthew, we went to the theater near the Blue
Ridge Mall and saw that movie. It was his choice. We sat in the very
front row, and when the horses ran across the screen, it felt like
they were stampeding over us! We will always miss our Matthew.

Yes, Jane, they do allow us limited visiting here, but it's such a
hassle that it would be best for you to wait until we land somewhere more permanent. I'll let you know.

From the news we're getting, this flood is devastating. My heart
goes out to the families who are homeless now. And cleanup will
be overwhelming. A crew of girls who are low security have been
going out to help sandbag.

Temporary phones have been strung in the hallways behind the
gym, but there are so many of us that we must wait in line for a
very long time to get a turn. I finally called home yesterday.

Unfortunately, the quality of the sound is not the best, but it
was great to hear your Grandma's sweet voice. When she informed
me that Betsy had given birth to my great-niece, I asked the baby's
name. It sounded like Grandma answered, "Potpourri."

"Potpourri? What kind of name is that, Momma?"

"I think it's a perfectly fine name."

"Oh, it's fine, don't get me wrong. Betsy can name her baby
anything she wants. It's just that I've never heard of anyone ever
named Potpourri."

"Well, I have."

"You have? Who?"

Grandma went into a long-winded story about some distant family member I'd never heard of before.

"So, your great aunt's cousin's grandma on Grandpa's side was named Potpourri?"

"Yes, and you remember Mary's friend Faith? One of her sisters was named Hope, but I never knew her middle name."

"HOPE!"

"Yes, Hope."

"The baby's name is Hope?"

"I TOLD you that! HOPE MARIE!"

I replied, "Oh, never mind—Momma, Hope Marie is so much better than Potpourri."

"No, Patty, the baby's name IS Hope Marie. I just told you that...."

Monday, July 19, 1993

Dear Mary,

The gym floor has wall-to-wall army cots, so many that it's difficult to maneuver between them. I wake up in the morning with my face only a few inches from my neighbor. These are close quarters.

Last night I heard a commotion from the hall behind the gym and looked up from my book just in time to see a covey of girls madly racing through the obstacle course. Screaming bloody murder. I swear, they never touched the ground.

Renee leaped on her cot and dove under the sheet. None of what she said made a bit of sense—just hysterical ranting—and when she'd poke her head out, her wild eyes would dart back to the doorway from whence she came.

In a blink of the eye, 200 half-asleep sweltering women, who were only hoping to feel a bit of a breeze from a fan, turned into petrified potential prey with absolutely no place to hide. Every lady, young and old alike, screamed with such high-pitched vigor that we sounded like a fleet of ambulance sirens.

It turned out that a group of male inmates had tried to break into our area—and pushed so hard on the big door that it actually gave way. The men literally fell in—practically on top of the card-playing girls who all had heart attacks and scattered.

The women who couldn't run away reported to me that our guards also suffered heart attacks when the guys broke in. With ashen faces our guards figured they'd have to brawl with those big bad boys, but in reality, the boys weren't that bad and scrambled back to their side. They even slammed the door behind them. As if it never happened.

Sometimes working for a goal is fun, but when you get what you thought you wanted, it's not really what you wanted. Either that or the guys chickened out.

When the threat was over, I had to laugh at Tammy, a big boyish Black girl. When the bad boys broke in, she immediately grabbed dainty Laura's feminine, flowered housecoat and wrestled feverishly in an attempt to cover her plus-size masculine form. Her explanation is that guys rape the obvious lesbians first.

The gym didn't calm down for some time. Just like a chicken house when foxes break in.

Friday, July 21, 1993

Dear Mary,

Did you notice that I have yet another address change? Renz has been deemed unsalvageable. Yesterday morning we packed up our meager belongings and trudged about a mile from the men's gym at Church Farm to a small work release prison on the back side of that prison.

The male inmates who resided in this facility obviously did not want to leave and protested in the grossest way imaginable. They urinated and defecated on the mattresses and all over the place—like animals.

You should have seen our collective disgusted expressions. Renz was bad in December '89 when we arrived there, but this is a whole new level of degradation. Fresh human waste is a strong sign—not just because of the sight and smell of it, but also for the demeaning cruel message it sent. Gag a maggot.

The staff expected us to just walk in and be grateful to have a place to reside. Any place. That shows how little they know about women. Instead, we screamed like scalded cats. We hollered at the top of our lungs, demanding cleaning supplies, disinfectant, shovels, scrub brushes, rags, mops.

Some tackled the unbelievably stinky showers. The irk-green slimy residue was almost pulsating as if alive. In fact, I think it was. Like the Blob. They used putty knives and scraped off thick layers of moldy crud. More than a dozen five-gallon bucket loads of that substance were hauled out of our dorm alone.

I won't go into the loads of fresh waste we removed. Mary, you really don't want to know about that. But we did mop the slick shitty floors more than twenty times before the water didn't resemble manure mud.

Because we're the strongest of body and stomach, Renee and I hauled the ruined mattresses out of the sally port. We did our level best to salvage the ones we could, because we had to make do. There would be no other beds or mattresses brought in as replacements.

At 10 pm Renee and I were still searching for rusted metal bed parts and fitting them together. Officer Wilson patiently escorted us on a hundred trips to the junk heap at the other end of the alley.

Around midnight we were finally all horizontal in relatively clean beds, exhausted except Betty who spent the entire night smashing crunchy-coated roaches against the walls with her shower shoes.

This morning when we arose and looked out the windows, Renee remarked that this prison looks like a cheap Tijuana motel. It does.

There are six telephone booths in a row outside. This little concrete block, peach-painted prison consists of five separate big rooms (dorms) on one side of an alley and the kitchen, administration, visiting room, canteen, etc. on the other side. Wonder how long we will be warehoused here? Sigh.

Friday, August 13, 1993

Dearest Sade,

Today Jane celebrates her twenthy-fourth birthday—and you will turn twenty-two in a couple of weeks. Mommas always say this, but it DOES seem like just yesterday you two were chubby, happy babies in diapers. Now you are both beautiful young women. I'm so proud.

Oh, I must tell you my most recent prison miracle. When we had to leave our belongings at Renz because of the flood, I left my only photo of Matthew in my Bible. There was no room in my pillowcase for unnecessary or fragile items.

Right after we bugged out, a maintenance man proudly informed me that he'd hefted my standup locker to safety up on my top bunk before Renz went under water. Then a few weeks after that, he came to me with his head down and was loath to tell me that the force of the surging swollen Mississippi River had knocked my bunk over, causing my locker to fall into the water. None of my belongings would be salvageable.

Sade, I acted like it was no big deal. Butch felt badly enough, but actually I was heartsick that I had lost the one-of-a-kind Polaroids of Matthew from our PATCH visits. Also, after Matthew died, Sister Monica, a sweet elderly Irish nun, sent me a small silver medal with a bleeding heart carved into one side and Mary crying at the feet of her crucified son on the other. That medal personifies my grief as much as any object can. I regretted not packing them with me.

A crew of staff and low-custody inmates recently boated out to our old, ruined dorm to get what they could. When the truckload of lockers arrived, Renee and I helped unload. Butch, the maintenance man, was right. My locker had been completely immersed in polluted flood water for way too long. Nothing could be saved.

Then Butch appeared grinning ear to ear holding my Bible. When my bed and locker fell into the river, the Bible had somehow slid into another bunk and remained high and dry through the whole disaster.

My photos are safe. The medal Sister Monica sent is safe. All I could do was stand there with my mouth open and tears in my eyes while clutching my remarkable Bible full of memories.

Thursday, March 10, 1994

Dear Marsha,

Since we don't have our own "liberry" (that's how it's pronounced by a great many in here) and chapel at this makeshift little prison, we use the men's facilities on certain nights. Currently my job is to keep the law library running smoothly.

Last month, I was busy typing up a divorce petition when my friend Helen appeared. As soon as I saw her white-strained face, I knew she needed to talk. After quickly excusing myself from my "client," I grabbed Helen's hand and whisked her into one of the Education offices so we could have some privacy.

I knew she had seen the Parole Board panel that day—which is a big, big major deal for those of us who serve no-parole sentences.

Helen had been serving life with no parole for fifty years until November '92, when Governor John Ashcroft commuted her sentence. The day we got that news we all rode on a great big emotional roller coaster!

Three of my sister inmates, Helen, Carlene, and Becca, who had been convicted of involvement in the murder of their abusive husbands and received no-parole sentences, were in the running for executive clemency, but only two were chosen. The third evidently didn't present enough proof of her husband's life-threateningly violent treatment to convince the panel that she qualified. All three lived in my dorm—the honor dorm. I was wildly thrilled for the two and sorely disappointed for the third.

Everyone thought the press would jump on the story of these executive clemencies, but only the Jefferson City paper ran a story as far as I know. If the *St. Louis Post-Dispatch* mentioned it, it was just that—a mention. No front-page bold print. Hardly a soul in the free world cared that the governor of our state had decided to wield his mighty sword of law-given executive power, and right a couple of injustices involving battered women. But inside the razor-wire fence of Renz, we celebrated.

When Helen received the commutation, she immediately became eligible to interview with the Parole Board. They gave her an interview date about fifteen months away, because we were told the governor wanted her to serve no less than thirteen years. This year makes thirteen.

Helen came to the law library that night to share her Parole Board experience. Her two stepchildren had attended the hearing in the role of victims—much to Helen's surprise. She hadn't seen them since she had come to prison and hardly recognized them. Can you imagine how difficult it would be to face the children of the man you had murdered—no matter what the reason? I can't.

Much to her credit, Helen had been a very loving and attentive stepmother, and these now-grown kids had nothing negative really to bring to the meeting. Just the fact that they appeared at the hearing in opposition to her parole hurt her heart. But that trip was probably not their idea.

Although Helen had an almost perfect prison record, the whole interview was extremely stressful and emotionally draining, and as Helen told me all about it, she cried. Helen doesn't fall apart easily either.

Petite Helen with her lush mane of curly blonde hair has lived a fascinating life story full of obstacles, adventures, horror, heartbreaks, and triumphs. She and her family fled from their native Yugoslavia when Helen was young and came to America. Can you imagine running away to a country where you couldn't speak the language and everything was strange? Needless to say, Helen has been through a great deal in her life.

In the middle of our conference in the Education office, Ted, our good ole hog farmer guard, lumbered in, took one look at me crying while I hugged and comforted a weeping Helen, turned right around, and beat a hasty retreat. He's a sweet country boy and obviously didn't want anything to do with blubbering females.

Not long after that nerve-racking hearing, Helen received the Board's order. She is slated to parole to an honor center (kind of a halfway house) in St. Louis. ASAP!

I forgot to mention that Helen's daughter, Becky, was only five when Helen had to leave her. Becky, who looks just like Helen except her hair is a gorgeous red, is now a young lady—and soon will be reunited with her mother in the free world. I get goosebumps when I think of going home to my now-grown children.

I'm so happy for her. Helen actually caught lightning in a jar. IT CAN BE DONE!

Friday, April 29, 1994

Dearest Momma and Daddy,

This is my anniversary—the eighth anniversary of my incarceration. It seems much longer than that. It seems as if I've been gone for a hundred years.

Since I took over Helen's PATCH job when she left, I have had so much fun with the kids in the visiting room. June and I arrange and finagle so that kids can get here to see their mothers. Does my heart good.

Yesterday a freckle-faced five-year-old boy named Dalton asked me why his mother was in prison. His serious, sincere blue eyes required a valid answer, so I told him that his mother had done something she wasn't supposed to and was in time-out. I asked if he'd ever heard of time-out, and he had. His nursery school teacher uses that technique to discipline.

I explained that in big-person time-out, we can't just sit in the corner. We have to come here to really think about what we've done—and the bad choices we've made.

I went on to make sure he knew that his mommy is a good person just like he is. But even good people sometimes make wrong decisions and need some time-out. And soon she will come home again.

Dalton seemed satisfied with the answer, because he hugged

and kissed me a sticky good-bye before he raced off to jump into his mother's lap.

When I give my weekly orientation talk to the brand-new girls, I tell them to use the time-out explanation for their little kids. Also, I advise them to be honest with the older ones. Kids know. They overhear everything. As Grandma always said, "Little pictures have big ears." (What exactly did that mean, Daddy?) Their kids know that they aren't away at college.

The main gist of my message is that our children are the biggest gift in our life and our biggest responsibility. I urge them to write their kids as much as possible—and write about real stuff, call them if their family can afford it, and sign up for PATCH visits. Maintaining contact with our children is so important—the most important thing we can do.

Usually I have them in tears, which is my goal. I want them to think about their kids and what they were doing instead of taking care of their kids. I want them to hurt so much they never forget their kids again.

With my words, I hope to grab them by the shoulders and shake them into reality. When I'm done, they know they've been lectured. No punches are pulled. I've heard every excuse imaginable as to why a woman can't nurture her kids from inside the fence of prison. None of them fly with me.

But the best part of my job is actually talking to and playing with the children who come here. Each one is special and beautiful in his or her own way. Sometimes they have me laughing and crying at the same time!

Momma and Daddy, you two have always been my role models for love. You raised us in love—unconditional love. I love you both with all my heart and am incredibly proud to be your first-born baby girl.

May 12, 1994

Dear Mary,

A couple of days ago, I went to the hole for "sexual misconduct."
That's what the guard wrote the violation as: sexual.

It all started the other night as I was coming in from the recreation yard. Renee, who has been locked up since she was about
fifteen, for the last fifteen years, was crying about her mother.
Something hurtful said between them. We know well how some
mothers can heap guilt on daughters without even trying.

Anyway, as I walked across the yard, Renee approached me
sobbing and blubbering, and I did what any friend would do. I
wrapped an arm around her shoulders and hugged her in sympathy. Our friend Mickie, who had just returned to prison for the
hundredth time (it seems) hugged her, too, on the other side. As
we exited the yard, we three old prison friends walked together
several feet with our arms around each other before parting to go
our separate ways. We live in three separate dorms.

Later as I prepared to hit the shower—we must bring everything we need with us to the shower—the yard guard stopped
at my cubicle and tersely ordered me to get my inmate ID card
and come with him. I knew I was in trouble but had no idea what
kind. It turned out that he had written a big fat conduct violation
accusing me of having sexual relations with Renee as we walked
back to the housing unit.

Gangster Shorty, the old-time sergeant who read the violation,
couldn't even look me in the eye. She'd known me since I set foot
in prison and knew it was bogus. Plus, even if I was going to have
sex, I wouldn't do it on the yard a few feet from two guards. But
sergeants ride with their officers.

The prison rule states that we are not to have any physical contact with anyone. We know that rule, but we break it all the time.
Can't help but break it. People need praise or comfort: a pat on
the back for a job well done, a hug when a loved one dies. Most
guards are smart enough and kind enough to recognize the different kinds of touch.

The whole prison squawked about Renee and me and this stupid conduct violation—staff and inmates alike. One male guard told me that the officer who wrote us up "had a hard-on" for me. I think that means he doesn't like me. Mickie wrote a witness statement explaining that she was also hugging Renee, so it was hardly fair for two of us to go down when three were involved— just because the guard is "cool" with Mick.

When Renee went to the caseworker for our hearing, we both were judged guilty and sentenced to ten days in the dreaded hole as punishment. We slowly made our way back to our separate dorms—still in disbelief—when it hit me that my family had planned to come visit me over the weekend.

Before we go to the hole, each pathetic inmate must pack up all her belongings and drag them to storage. After I sorted and shuffled and stuffed everything I own in a couple of cardboard boxes, no guard arrived to take me away, so I called Momma, "I hate to have to tell you this, but you can't visit me this weekend. Renee and I are going to the hole for ten days—and I can't have any visits while I'm down there."

Typically, and ever the optimist, Momma replied, after looking for the silver lining, "Oh well, you two girls will have fun together...."

"Momma, I'm sure we won't be in the same cell. They say that we were having sex. Together. With each other. That's the reason for the violation. That's why we're going to the hole."

"WHAT? SEX! WITH EACH OTHER! ARE THEY ALL CRAZY?"

Since I had her full attention, I gave her a brief rundown. Momma quickly decided that she must call the superintendent. "What kind of people are these? No one in their right mind would have sex out there while everyone was watching! What kind of rule is it that you can't hug someone when she's crying? Can't they tell the difference in the kinds of touches? Don't they have hearts? Renee is just a young girl. I gotta call." Click. Momma hung up on me.

All I could do was sit and wait for the officer to return and cuff me for the long walk to the hole. The hole here is in the men's prison and not only nasty and disgusting with an open toilet in the cell, but the men inmates can peep our every move through the bars. I've heard horror stories, and sadly it looked like I would soon glean firsthand knowledge.

Adventure. I was trying to think of this as just another prison adventure.

And I was loath to have a stinkin' "sexual misconduct" stuck in my file. Not that I'm scheduled to see the parole board for a consideration hearing in the next four decades, but I have never even looked at a woman, any woman, in a sexual way. I have nothing against that way of being—it's just not my way. In the same vein, I'd hate to have a stealing violation in my file, too, because I'm no thief.

Well, I waited and waited. Stewing in the juice of apprehension. Simmering in the pot of dread. Count was called. Chow was called. Still no word.

Sometime in late afternoon, an old-time friendly guard, who was ambling his security-check rounds, noticed me still perched on my box and advised, "Hey, gal. Didn't ya hear? Your trip to the Bahamas was canceled. You need to unpack. I can't believe nobody told you."

Thank you, Momma! As soon as my meager belongings were safe in my locker and my bunk was remade, I phoned her. Yes, she did call the superintendent and somehow persuaded him to use common sense and overrule the caseworker's sentence. Whew!

Saturday, September 17, 1994

Dear Nancy,

I broke my foot. Yep. I can't believe it either. Remember when I accidentally sailed my bike off the bridge between our homes on Easley Road? I didn't break anything then—not even the bike. From all the tumbles I've taken in my tomboy life, no bones ever fractured. But here I am with a broken foot getting around on these tools-of-torture aptly named crutches. Even the word sounds painful: crutches. Say it out loud. Ca-rutch-es. I hate them.

All I did was attempt to climb down from my top bunk while holding a mug full of soda pop. No differently than the other ten million times I've successfully accomplished that feat. To reach the ground, I have to first swing my feet down into a metal folding chair. As a make-shift chair cushion, Mickie had folded a percale sheet. My feet slid on the sheet and BAM, I fell hard on my back, bouncing my noggin on the concrete floor and knocking the breath out of me.

Reminded me of that time when a gang of us high schoolers played crack-the-whip during an ice skating party, and I ended up as the tail of the whip and was cracked so hard that I flew way up and then crashed on the unforgiving ice of your pond. Same feeling. Same embarrassment, too.

When I opened my eyes and blinked, all my neighbors were peering down at me—the easily excitable were screaming for an officer. I laid down there for a moment collecting my wits—which I later found were spilling out the back of my head—and realized that I was still holding the mug and hadn't spilled a drop. I'm pretty proud of that accomplishment, too.

Before I could stand up, a sergeant appeared scowling. Officers really hate hurt inmates. That means paperwork. I sat up and touched the back of my aching head to find the oozy warmth of blood. Rats! I'd split my head open. I envisioned a big ugly shaved spot.

I kept telling everyone I was fine and tried to joke that with my hard head I fell on the strongest part of me. Someone helped me to my feet—and that's when I first realized that my right foot hurt. Hurt bad!

The sergeant ordered me to walk to medical. I begged for mercy—but he remained unmoved. Paperwork must be done, and it would be better for him if someone else did it. The nurse decided that since this was a head injury, I must spend the night in the infirmary for observation. OH! NO! NOT THE INFIRMARY! I pleaded like a person heading for the gallows!

The infirmary is not in our prison camp. Oh no, the infernal infirmary is in the men's prison at Fulton. Horror stories of that place have been told too many times for me to ignore. I felt like hanging on the door jamb and wailing like a little kid who refused to be left at daycare.

My state gray uniform was sent for. We only wear uniforms when leaving the prison. I was also strip searched. Can't travel without that. My foot, by this time, was swollen and throbbing, but the officer forced me to don my shoes. She kept telling me that my head was the wounded part. Guess she never heard of anyone injuring more than one part at a time.

Fulton is about thirty miles away, I believe, but the trip took forever! My foot pain was excruciating in that tight shoe. The place is a fortress with many checkpoints. By the time we arrived at my observation cell, tears were in my eyes. The first thing I did, before the nurse strip searched me, was wrestle the right shoe off my screaming foot. (OK, if my foot COULD have screamed, it would have.)

The nurse handed me a thin state gown, took my clothes and my vitals, and left. I never saw her again, although I was there for observation. Turned out, the male inmates took care of that chore. The skinny Black guy, who was mopping the floor outside my glass-walled cell, never took his eyes off me. The floor outside my cell was so clean I bet the paint suffered. And he must have alerted his friends.

Remember the reptile house at the zoo where the creatures are kept in glass cages so that visitors are entertained by the captive reptile's every move? That's exactly how this was. And I was the unfriendly exotic lizard that everyone just had to see.

Also, the male officer, whose station was right outside my observation cell, kept an eye on me. All this attention would not have been so horrendous if the toilet was not in the cell with me. Right out there in the middle of the room with no screen or privacy of any kind.

Finally, in desperation after I'd figured out the timing of the men's comings and goings and when they both left, I pushed a blanket-covered chair in front of the commode as a pathetic shield and used the facility as quickly as womanly possible. This fast maneuver was done while hopping on one foot as I could no longer put weight on the black-and-blue one. Just as I pulled up my panties, the mopper returned to leer at me.

The next morning, a female guard escorted me to x-ray. Thankfully she was good natured and allowed me to hop down the hall. After the tech had taken pictures of my head, I asked for a foot x-ray, too. His answer was, "I can't, Mrs. Prewitt, my orders are for the head only."

That was the last blasted straw—the straw that broke the broken-footed camel's back. Or something like that. I muled down on the table and absolutely refused to leave without a foot x-ray. The young tech nervously looked for help from our guard. She sided with me. After my foot was x-rayed, the tech poked his head out from behind the lead barrier and proclaimed, "Your foot is broken."

"OK, now can I STOP squeezing my foot into those shoes?"

When the Renz guard arrived to take me home, I could have kissed her. Stripping quickly for the perfunctory search, I couldn't wait to get out of that place with the glassed observation cell and all the male inmates and staff attention. She even acquired a wheelchair to roll me the thousand miles of hall before we found our van.

Upon arrival back at my prison, a nurse appeared in the sally port and handed me crutches. The guard taught me how to use them on our way to the strip search area. (Did you notice how many strip searches I danced through during this odyssey?)

The x-ray tech had allowed me to view the foot photo, so I could see which bone was broken and how. When I settled back in at my dorm, I placed a ball of cotton, salvaged from a vitamin bottle, between my little toe and its neighbor and taped the two together. I figured that would lever the broken bone back where it belongs to heal. One of my friends gave me a small ace bandage, which was perfect to secure the rest of my foot, and she examined and cleaned my head wound, which had been looked at by no one since I first fell.

It's a good doggone thing my friends and I took care of this ourselves, because it was a week before I saw a doctor—not that it did any good. The prison doctor couldn't find the x-ray, so he didn't do anything. In prison, we learn how to doctor ourselves.

Superintendent Goeke stopped by PATCH and asked about my foot. When he heard that they hadn't even given me a bootie to protect it, he called medical and had a German fit. Before the end of the day, I sported a blue bootie on my fractured foot.

The worst part of this is the crutches. The skin under my arms—both inside my arm and outside my rib cage—has worn off. Seriously. Four open wounds have developed. But my arms look really good! You should see my muscular deltoids.

And I am fast as can be on them—I even cruise the track. Bet I could win a crutches race. Even though I HATE crutches. I even hate the sound of the word. Crutches. Sounds tortuous, doesn't it? Ca-rutch-es.

Monday, January 16, 1995

Dear Nancy,

Yesterday my sweet folks traveled across the state to visit me. After I was strip searched and finally made my way to them for our greeting hugs and kisses, Momma furtively inquired, "Patty, do you know that couple over there?" I did. The wife lived in my dorm.

In hushed tones, Momma leaned forward and observed, "Her husband is so odd. We stand in line with him practically every time we come here, but he never talks. You know I can get ANYONE to talk, but not him. He just seems so sad. What's his wife in here for?"

"Attempted murder. She tried to kill him."

Daddy, who had been listening intently, snorted, "Well! That'd wipe the smile off your face!"

June 14, 1995

Dear Nancy,

Today Morgan turned eighteen, which means this was the last PATCH visit for which we qualify. June, the PATCH lady, brought in a special cake for the celebration. All my kids and grandkids traveled here for the party: Janie, Zachary, Jace, Sade, Carrie, and Morgan.

Zach and Jace are so cute with June. She wears quite a bit of makeup and jewelry, so in their eyes she's just beautiful. Once six-year-old Zach told his mother that he wished she would get fixed up like Aunt June. These boys like flash!

Three-year-old Jace suggested to Jane that they buy me a purse. His theory is that if I had a purse, I could come home. All free ladies have purses. Oh, and a car. According to Jace, if they would chip in and buy me a purse and a car, I'd visit their house. Sure wish it were that simple.

The little boys think I live with June. When I was housed at old Renz, Zach told his mother that I lived on a "boat" with Aunt June. We guess he thought the trailer was a dry-docked ship of sorts. He also thought we slept together on the couch, since there was no bed there. Zach tried to persuade his mother to allow him to sleep on the couch, too.

Did I tell you about Easter weekend when Jane and her little family visited? When it was time for me to dress as the Easter Bunny, I excused myself from the table and changed in the bathroom. When I reappeared in my white furry bunny glory, Jace hollered, "It's the Easter Bunny! Where's Granny? She's missing him!"

I played for hours with my boys and all the other kids. Right before visiting hours were over, Jane helped me change back. As soon as Jace saw me emerge from the bathroom, he yelled, "Granny! You missed the Easter Bunny! Where were you?"

That bunny story reminds me of another. When Zach attended kindergarten in Louisiana, his teacher called Janie in about his apparent problem with reality and telling the truth. Janie was just sick—any young first-time mother would be. Then the teacher told Jane that Zach had shared with his class that not only was his grandmother in prison, she was the Easter Bunny. Jane breathed a sigh of relief and informed the teacher that Zach was not telling a fib. It was true!

During the final PATCH visit, Carrie and Sade discussed college. Morgan talked about finding work. Janie talked about the joys of motherhood. The whole day was a celebration, not only of Morgan's birth, but of the amazing love we share.

After we hugged and kissed emotional and tearful goodbyes, I stepped into the strip search room. That's when the guard screwed up her mouth and accused, "Mrs. Prewitt, you are much, much too affectionate with your children."

Drawing my naked self up to my full height, I struggled to remain calm but very firmly advised, "When I die, I hope that's EXACTLY what is carved in my gravestone: SHE WAS TOO AFFECTIONATE WITH HER CHILDREN. I hope everyone on this earth accuses me of that. And I will always be affectionate with my children no matter how old they get. No matter what."

She let loose a piggy snort, but that was the end of the discussion.

August 23, 1995

Dear Mary,

Did I ever tell you that I sleep near a cannibal?

Supposedly, short, stout, blonde-headed Vicki, who resembles a cross between Alf and W. C. Fields, and her boyfriend murdered people and ate them. Not at the kill site, I don't believe. The duo butchered their victims and froze the prime cuts—at least that's what I've been told.

No, I'm not making this up. My fertile imagination is not THAT creative. She's serving twenty years or so for those meals. Shoulda become a vegetarian instead. Janie could have given her some meatless recipes. Also, Vicki likes to say that white people taste like cheese and Black people taste like chicken.

The reason I mention my cannibal Alf is because today it was brought to our attention that she needs a shower. Vicki must be part cat. She is not at all fond of water. (Personally, the shower is the best-feeling activity left in prison for me.) The worst part of dealing with Vicki is that her IQ is about the same as her shoe size, poor girl. (I started to compare her IQ to her dress size but realized that would be way too generous.)

When the temperature reaches 100 in the dorm, tempers flare— especially when the stench of an occupant affects everyone. The job of unstinking Vicki fell to Mickie and me, because we were the most liable to get it done peacefully.

Mick ended up practically in the shower with Vick. When we first sent her in, she was back out in a few seconds and not even damp. So Mickie closely monitored the cleaning while I stood safely outside the shower standing bust.

Now the occupants of 4-Dorm are happy—for the time being. This type of solution doesn't last long in this heat though. Especially since Vicki's favorite activity is to dance to head-banging heavy metal music on her Walkman. Honestly, I get a kick out of watching her uninhibitedly groove to the loud music, but our resident cannibal will soon require another shower.

According to prison lore, Em, an intelligent but a bit off-center Black lady, sawed off her father's head and toted it in a bowling ball bag—the perfect size for that purpose. She and I are cool, but I have witnessed indications that there is a side to her that might actually pull off such a stunt. She's serving twenty or twenty-five, I'm not sure.

Just think, if I hadn't fallen into this strange land, like Alice through the looking glass, you'd never hear firsthand accounts of all these incredible characters who populate our prison. And the strangest aspects of these stories is that these criminally insane individuals are slated to parole in a few years. They get a second chance, but I don't. This is certainly a very strange land.

November 22, 1995

St. Louis Post-Dispatch Editorial Section
"Cruel and Inhumane Treatment"

Letter to the Editor,

On November 8, after lunch, everyone in the honor dorm at Renz Correctional Facility was told to stay in until we had a lice check. No one was concerned. We've done this hundreds of times. A nurse from the Health Center found two cases of head lice.

Shortly after that, a guard announced that we were to send all our clothing and bedding to the neighboring men's prison to be laundered. We were to strip, be deloused with a chemical shampoo, then wear thin paper gowns until the clothes were returned.

As can be imagined, we balked. Most of us had clothes stolen (panties, especially) and ruined by the men's laundry during our stay there in the Great Flood of '93. Also, we all know how transparent paper gowns are. Most of the guards here are male.

We asked to speak to the associate superintendent. Instead, more male guards arrived to threaten us. We still insisted on speaking to the associate superintendent. This was not the first lice infestation at Renz and never before had we had to do anything so drastic. Finally, a group of us were allowed to meet with the associate superintendent, the head nurse, and several guards. They told us right away that the E-Squad was waiting to mace and strip us forcibly. We knew the older, sick ladies could not endure that pain and humiliation. The only concession given to us was to be able to store our good clothes for two weeks in lieu of laundering them by the men.

So, we trudged back to the dorm with heavy hearts and started packing. The next few hours were a blur of sorting, bagging, marking, and carrying bags. After dinner we began the slow process of delousing, five at a time. After the lice treatment, we were put in paper gowns. We also cut head and arm holes in big trash bags to wear for modesty and warmth.

The unfortunate ladies on their menstrual cycles pleaded for panties because sanitary napkins must stick to something. They were offered used panties from another dorm. For obvious reasons, they turned down that offer. I suggested to the lieutenant that the clothing room be opened so new panties could be secured. She said that was a good idea and left to check. That was as far as that went.

Later I pleaded with several guards to go to the clothing room to get sheets, blankets, anything for the ladies to put on to get warm. I was told that no one had a key to that area. I know that a set of master keys are under glass. In emergencies the glass is broken. I told the officer to "break the glass." He looked horrified that I even knew the "secret" and left.

The ladies who had been "treated" for lice were in no way separated from the "untreated." In fact, those who are given medication and had to go to the Health Center in their bags ended up mingling with untreated women from other dorms. By 2 am all fifty-three ladies in my dorm were in garbage bags with wet hair, so the dorm lights were switched off.

As we lay on our bare plastic mattresses on steel bunks in a concrete building, we huddled in our individual trash bags, shivering against the cold, praying for strength. A heavy, silent fog of sadness settled over the dorm. As exhausted as we were, no one could sleep. We could only lay alone in the chilly darkness listening to the rustle of our neighbors' trash bags. We all felt forlorn and brokenhearted.

Between 4:30 and 5 am the bank of fluorescent dorm lights was unceremoniously flicked on. Our laundry was here. Stiffly we climbed off our hard bunks to begin the three-hour process of finding our own clothes and bedding.

We want everyone to know exactly how we were tortured. Even if you despise us for the sole reason that we are in prison, you surely see that this was wrong and inhumane.

November 25, 1995

Dearest Nancy,

As a grade school teacher, I KNOW you have plenty of lice-related stories, but I bet you and your students never spent the night in trash bags!

The *St. Louis Post-Dispatch* printed my letter to the editor a few days ago—and the lice hit the fan. The whole delousing plan was handled so ineptly and insanely that I would not believe it if I hadn't experienced it!

The prison nurse found only two cases of suspected head lice. Later I checked Leigh and found she didn't even have lice. I KNOW lice. Carrie afforded me the opportunity of becoming an expert when she was in kindergarten. The other lady was infested but had repeatedly asked the Health Center for help. This was not new to her or us.

The morning after our lousy night, I heard an older arthritic lady sob on the phone as she told her son how she'd been humiliated and how cold she'd been all night in nothing but a paper gown and trash bag in a drafty dorm in the dead of winter. For the last twelve hours, I'd been so busy trying to take care of my friends, trying to survive, that I had not stepped back and realized how inhumanely we were treated throughout the process—from the first moment when the guards threatened to forcibly strip us. There was NO reason to herd and dip us like lousy, diseased sheep.

Anger rose up in me when I saw that sweet elderly woman crying to her son and describing her night. What do I do when I get mad? I pull out my mighty sword, my Bic pen, and slay the dragon—or scribble.

In that letter to the editor, I didn't even describe the whole night. For example, the next morning when work details were announced, our guard, a tall skinny kid, ordered us to go to work right that minute. Most of the ladies were still in trash bags searching for their clothes.

The laundry had washed everything in a couple of big loads. Can you imagine a dayroom, knee-deep in wadded-up laundry, and fifty-three trash-bag-clad, sleep-deprived, cold, mad women wading through the mess? A wild, frenzied Kmart blue-light special is a cakewalk compared to that scene.

The guard was so incensed when the mob blatantly disregarded his order that he shouted, "THERE WILL BE REPERCUS-SIONS!" Don't know what else he said because his shouts were drowned out by a chorus of irate bagged ladies hurling obscenities. This particular guard is now known as "Mr. Repercussions Man."

I grew up in an old drafty wood frame farmhouse, but I don't ever remember feeling so cold. When it was time to get to bed, I balled myself up so tightly in my bag that I had trouble unfurling. By rubbing my bare feet with my hands, I attempted to thaw them. We all were miserable. I heard the sobs of my equally pathetic neighbors in the dark.

Still, I can hardly believe that we were forced to spend the night in nothing but transparent thin paper gowns, like the ones doctors give to barely cover yourself for three minutes during an exam, and plastic trash bags. Nothing else. Nothing. No bedding. No socks. No undies. Nothing.

And we wouldn't have had the trash bags if we hadn't taken the bull by the horns and demanded them. In fact, clear transparent trash bags were first offered to us by the male guards. Every male guard on camp was in our dorm keeping a close eye on the women who wore only see-through, open-in-the-front-or-back paper gowns, which closed and fastened with only one tie. I'm sure we were under personal surveillance in the name of security. Until black bags were delivered for us to use for modesty and a bit of warmth, we had a hissy fit.

Every time I think about that night, I either feel mad or hurt all over again. But I understand my letter to the editor was picked up by several newspapers across the state. Hopefully, the bad press will prevent the Department of Corrections from hosting another "Lice Festival."

I can feel your concern for me already. Don't worry. I only told the truth. What can they do to me for telling the truth? If I'm punished, I'll write another letter to the editor about THAT!

I cannot keep quiet out of fear. That's what they expect from the incarcerated, but it's not in me.

Oh, yes, we named that night the "Lice Festival of 1995." As a defense mechanism, inmates find humor in the sorriest experiences.

May 11, 1996

Dear Governor Mel Carnahan:

During the past ten years that I've been in prison, I've talked to, counseled with, and assisted many ladies who have committed some form of murder, whether by themselves or in cahoots with another. One common factor for almost every one of these women is the lack of family closeness and trust.

Most have been sexually abused by a close family member and were afraid to tell other family members. Most felt they could not go to a member of their family for help when their domestic situation soured or they were too deep in the wrong crowd. Most didn't even have a trusted friend to confide in. (I say "most" because I have seen a couple of women with manslaughter cases where the family was supportive, but the accident still occurred.)

My background is not at all like those at all. I was raised by a close family where my grandparents, parents, aunts, uncles, cousins, and siblings interacted daily. I was always confident that I could ask any family member for help. They would have even taken in the children and me if necessary. (Although I'm not saying my mother wouldn't have pestered me to patch things up with my husband, because she would have.)

I did not murder Bill Prewitt. I would never have murdered Bill Prewitt. At my very angriest, I always had an option to leave and go home to my loving parents. To me, that's a critical point to note.

Also, sir, not only am I blessed with loving parents, I am a loving parent. My children are precious gifts and serious responsibilities. I would never ever have traumatized them by murdering their beloved father only a few feet away from our young sleeping children. I have always gone to great lengths to shelter them. My husband and I both did.

Another commonality women in prison share is a lack of employability. Most had meager jobs at best, were not self-sufficient, and were financially as well as emotionally dependent on a man. That was far from the case with me. I was a realtor, had earned college credits, possessed bookkeeping and secretarial skills, was proficient in the hardware/building supply business, and would have easily found a good job if I had decided our marriage was beyond repair. On top of that, Bill Prewitt was a very good father and would have been generous with financial support for his children. Deadbeat dads are the norm for prison mothers.

I have also, from time to time through the years, heard the theory that I know who killed my husband but am afraid to tell. Another version on that theme is that I know who killed my husband but am protecting that individual. Good Lord! If I am anything in this world, I am open, opinionated, and unafraid to speak up. If I know anything more than what I've told every deputy sheriff and attorney who came around, I don't know what it could be. I've told all I know. I don't know who the man is who killed my husband. I wish with all my heart that I did.

Since I have been incarcerated, I have taken every college class and training possible. I have graduated from NMCC's business college, attended Trenton Junior College classes, earned an associate's degree from Lincoln University, studied NMCC's paralegal courses, and am currently training to be a computer applications programmer with the Information Systems Unit of the Department of Corrections. Prior to my incarceration, I was a solid, taxpaying citizen and will have no problem resuming that role if released.

Governor Carnahan, I pray that you will realize that what I say is true and will grant me the executive clemency that only you have the power to bestow. I promise you will never regret your decision should you choose to right this miscarriage of justice.

Thursday, July 25, 1996

Dear Marsha,

On occasion, I am so involved with my job, my mission to get out of prison, and my family that I forget exactly with whom I cohabitate. Not tonight.

After I speed-walked for an hour around the track, showered, and changed into nightclothes, I positioned myself cross-legged on my top bunk with my little fan aimed at me so I could settle in for the night and answer some letters. Pretty normal evening so far.

The girl who lives on the top bunk behind me remarked to no one in particular, "Wow! I think Sam just poured Kool-Aid on Bobby."

I turned to see what in the world she was talking about. Inmates aren't prone to pouring Kool-Aid on officers. Through the back window I could see Sam standing in front of Mr. A. The blood stain on the back of his uniform shirt was growing larger. Oh, my God! Sam had stabbed him.

By that time I'd hurried to the windows, all my silent and stunned neighbors were there. We watched Mr. A spray mace on Sam, who by this time was on her knees before him. He emptied the can on an unphased Sam. I used the word unphased because Sam knelt there at his feet as if in adulation with no emotion, no movement, no choking, no expression.

Pepper mace is a horrible substance. My eyes water if I get the slightest whiff, but Sam, whose face was wet and red with the stuff, never blinked.

The Neo-Nazi-looking and acting Mr. A is an ass in the truest sense of the word. In the fall of '92, he interrupted a special church service during a gospel concert and checked all of us for IDs. Carded the congregation. I'm serious. Marsha, the chapel was full of happy singing worshippers when Bobby kicked in the door like a DEA agent on a big drug bust.

Every one of us who did not have our inmate identification card on us got in trouble—I was one of them. I'd changed to my good jeans for church and left my ID in the other pants. After I received a CDV (conduct violation), I pointed out to the sergeant that at least now there was proof in my file that I did indeed attend church.

Now that I think about it, that story is probably an example of Bobby on his best behavior. He's a natural terror. Recently he actually maced the priest as he exited the chapel. Turns out that Father Behan knows a whole lot of impressive curse words. Some in Celtic, I believe.

Earlier this evening he and Sam had words. He's famous for egging on arguments—baiting the ones who will allow him to. Bobby always holds out the worm of confrontation on his irritating little hook. But he should NOT have thrown a line to a barracuda.

The girls tell me that they overheard him tell Sam, "If you feel froggy, leap." No one with good sense would ever give Sam that permission slip. No one ever accused Bobby of having good sense.

Sam broke down a disposable razor to retrieve the blade, melted the end of her toothbrush with a lighter, and welded the two together to make a common but effective prison weapon. Then she waited around for the best time and as Bobby stood outside the back door smoking. she saw her opportunity to teach him one of her prison lessons—the "Don't Forget Exactly Where You Are" lesson.

Earlier as I made my way to the shower area, I met her dressed in prison grays, pacing and chain-smoking roll-your-owns nervously. "Sam, what's going on? Going somewhere?" We only wear those hot uniforms if we're going beyond the fence. Sam just smiled unsteadily in answer. I smiled back. "Never disturb the disturbed" is my motto.

It's my understanding that Mr. A has a lot of stitches. Sam's in the hole. It's unnaturally quiet in here. Bloody displays of violence like that tend to make me feel sick and shaky. I'm probably not the only one. Bobby is a numbskull, but he didn't deserve to be slashed.

The first time I witnessed a woman actually try to kill another was a few years ago in the gym at old Renz. With a ceramic coffee cup, Ella beat her girlfriend in the head so hard and so many times that blood was splattered everywhere. In my mental photo album, I have saved a picture of Ella's blood-covered crazed face as she crouched over her victim—looking like a hungry black panther attacking a gazelle.

I was blithely exercising to a Kathy Smith aerobic video tape only a few feet away when I heard those dull thuds—the awful sound of a heavy mug hitting a hard skull. Bill, the recreation officer, had to grab my arm and force me away because I couldn't move. Frozen, I could only watch the horrible scene beside me. After I recovered a bit, I ran to the toilet, upchucked supper, and washed blood off my face.

Both staff and inmates are solemn tonight. We've had a heavy dose of reality. We remember where we are. We remember who lives here with us. And we mourn those brutal truths.

Wednesday, October 23, 1996

Dear Mary,

The shop in which I work is a big trailer that was pulled up behind the small prison. In fact, five trailers now sit behind my dorm. Medical, Classification, Education, Data Entry, and Information Systems Unit (me) use the double-wides.

Twelve of us work with ISU writing and analyzing computer programs for the Department of Corrections. The work is difficult and intense, and we use humor to break the tension now and then. We have evolved into practical jokers and teasers.

With the cool weather, field mice have naturally moved into the warm trailer. Everyone knows that I detest finding myself in the same room with a rodent—any rodent. Don't even like gerbils. I can hop up on my desk with the best of them. The girls still tease me about the time at old Renz when I unexpectedly found a field mouse trapped in a wastepaper can and leaped like Wonder Woman straight up and over about eight feet to a whole other cubicle.

But boyish blonde thirty-year-old Rox beats me by a mile. She's liable to hurt herself to get away from the tiniest mouse.

Not too long ago Rox was sitting on the throne in the toilet when a field mouse scurried across her feet. We heard a little-girl squeal and frantic thrashing, bumping noises before she finally jerked the door open and raced clear out of the trailer and down the sidewalk as fast as she could—which was pretty doggone fast considering her trousers were only halfway up.

The rest of us in the shop just sat at our respective workstations with our mouths open as Rox whizzed by. As soon as we found out what had prompted her erratic and frenzied behavior, we laughed until we cried. You would have thought Godzilla was in the little bathroom.

Lena fashioned a small realistic mouse for me out of felt and cotton stuffing. I keep it on top of my terminal—my mascot. Every computer nerd should have a mouse, right?

One day I looked up at my little gray mascot with the black thread whiskers, tiny French knot eyes, and long felt tail—and thought about Rox. I waited until she was exiting the bathroom, then I jumped up from my desk screaming, "Mouse! Aaaahhhh!" After setting the stage with award-winning acting, I tossed the stuffed rodent onto the already scared Rox.

The imitation mouse hit Rox square on the chest, and she dropped like it was a hand grenade. I mean she fell straight back, spread-eagled and landed on the floor hard—like a dead person! Boom! And she stayed there. Still as a mouse. None of us had ever seen anything like it.

For a moment, I feared I had actually stopped her heart and killed her! I think both Donna and Mickie peed their pants.

March 5, 1997

Dear Mary,

I just finished one of those odd exchanges that can only occur in prison.

Our dorm guard was walking around the dorm "conducting a routine security check," when he stopped at my cubicle, where I was hunkered over the architectural plans I'm drawing for maintenance, and pointed at my small plastic wastepaper can.

"Patty, that paper bag you've got in there is a fire hazard."

I peered into the can, "The paper bag is a fire hazard? What do I do with it?"

"Well, it can't be used as a liner. Just wad it up," he advised.

I reached in, balled up the bag, and tossed it into the same trash can. Then I asked, "So, if the bag is spread out around the perimeter of the can, it will burn. But if the bag is on the bottom or on this side or on that side or folded or wadded or shredded, it won't burn?"

He stood motionless. In fact, he didn't appear to breathe.

Taking his glassy-eyed silence as my green light, I continued, "What about the trash paper? Old letters? Wrappers? Must I place them in the can a certain way to be inflammable? In all my science classes, I've never learned the theory of the relationship between origami and fire. Of course, scientific theories change all the time. It's difficult to keep abreast of innovations and discoveries."

Our dorm guard slowly turned and walked away.

"Hey, officer, where you going? I want to know! Inquiring minds want to know. OK, you go on now, but if my granola bar wrapper spontaneously combusts, it's your fault!"

Sunday, November 16, 1997

Dear Nancy,

I try not to write you when I'm feeling this way, but Matthew would have turned twenty-four tomorrow, if he were still with us. I can't help but imagine what he'd be up to now. He would have graduated from college a few years ago and would probably be established in his chosen profession by now. He might even have a family. I can't dwell on coulda-beens. Can't let myself fall back into that deep, dark pit.

Recently the girls and I discussed Matthew's death. I still cannot believe that he took his own life. According to the girls, there were no signs of the kind of depression associated with suicide. He'd just graduated. His social life was active. None of it makes any sense. Daddy told me that the pistol was found in his left hand. Matt was right-handed.

Did you know that Daddy and Morgan found Matt's body tightly wrapped in a blanket near the creek? How awful. At first, they didn't even recognize that the young man they discovered was our Matt. Daddy still cries when we speak of the horror and loss of our dear Matthew. We all do. Morgan has yet to open up to me about his feelings. Even after five years, the memory is too painful.

My family holds Matthew's ashes in safekeeping so that when I come home we can have a ceremony together. That's the way the kids want it.

I just found out that my dear friend Michelle passed away Thursday. Although I knew it was inevitable, I still feel stunned. It didn't have to be that way.

After I met Michelle here at Renz, we soon discovered we were the same age, and both of us had gone off to different colleges the same year—she to KU. I took a liking to her right off the bat. Her Harley-biker, no-nonsense, straightforward demeanor and dry sense of humor tickled me. I'm not sure what her felony conviction was, but I do know she'd tried to harm her boyfriend—in some sort of domestic spat that got out of hand—as Jack Daniels-fueled biker battles commonly do.

When Michelle first showed symptoms that something was not right, the prison doctor swore she had internal hemorrhoids. When she passed out from the pain during a bowel movement, we knew the doc was wrong.

In prison it takes months and months to get medical attention— if ever. We fill out a Medical Services Request form and drop it in the box. Then in a day or two, a nurse sees us. A nurse's job is to weed out 99.9 percent of the sick applicants. Getting examined by a prison doctor is tough. But if you make it to one, the doctor's job is to weed out 99.9 percent of the applicants who made it through to him. It's all about money. The less money spent on medical care, the more money for the medical company to spend.

It took months before Michelle was sent out to the real world to see a real doctor. By then a huge malignant tumor had grown in her rectum. She suffered through painful surgeries, months of burning radiation, and the lethal poison of chemo. Not a whimper. Not a complaint. And every trip out for treatment meant handcuffs, shackles, and chains. She went through that terrible torture twice! The cancer came back.

When Michelle returned from her first surgery, she found her locker had been stocked with everything we could think of from the canteen. I was standing there beaming when she discovered her loot, so she accused me of doing it all—but I quickly ratted on my friends. All the women who live in our large open dorm contributed. Even those who have no money at all. The tough-acting biker chick, who has known so little of kindness and generosity in her life, broke down, covered her face with her hands, and sobbed.

She lost her beautiful long hair with the chemo. The honey-brown tresses fell out in clumps. Mickie spied her in the gang shower and stammered, "Ah, ah, ah, you, you have no hair anywhere, Michelle!"

We had to laugh, because Michelle retorted in her dry manner, "Well, hell, Mick, what part of NO HAIR don't ya understand!?"

This spring when my sister was here and Michelle was also in the visiting area, Mary started in again about how I should meet a yodeler she knows and how she is certain that we'd hit it off. From that day forward, Michelle teased me unmercifully about this musician friend of Mary's by performing horrible off-key mock-orgasmic yodeling that she knew embarrassed the daylights out of me.

When an inmate is certain to die, she is eligible for a medical parole. When Michelle won her approval papers, I came down with a bad case of mixed feelings. She wasn't going to die in prison, but she was going to die. Too soon.

She had no one but a teenage son in state custody, so the sweet McCurrens—the family who are taking care of an inmate's baby while she's in prison—offered to let her parole to them. How many people do you know who would take in a sick and dying, strange felon? Momma calls Rob and Paula angels on earth. She's right.

Michelle paroled to their loving home last summer.

The McCurrens allowed me to call and speak to Michelle, who invariably broke out that caterwauling yodel to tease and befuddle me. That would make her laugh when nothing else would. Recently her advancing illness prevented her from talking on the phone.

Michelle is no longer in pain. Her suffering has ended. She's free—totally free. But she's not gone from this plane of existence. She'll forever live in her son's heart, and in mine. When I think about strength and courage, her sweet face comes to mind. I wish you could have met her.

Sunday, November 30, 1997

Dear Nancy,

BULLETIN: This is unbelievable, but Governor Carnahan's chief counsel, Joe Bednar, is scheduled to interview me in a couple of weeks. The governor is sending him, plus one of those transcribers, to ask me questions in regard to my clemency application.

Nancy, this is the FIRST time a governor has ever gone this far for me. This is the first time anyone from the governor's office has ever asked to talk to me!

Remember Representative Dale Whiteside? I met him at Chillicothe years ago. Bless his heart, Dale is working hard to gain commutations for the five of us that he'd taken on. Dale was instrumental in gaining clemency for my friend Helen from Governor Ashcroft.

December 22, 1997

Dear Honorable Governor Mel Carnahan:

I had strict orders to call certain individuals after last week's meeting with Joe Bednar and Shelly Freund. So, after lunch but before I went back to work, I phoned my oldest daughter Jane. She and her sons reported to me that they lit candles and prayed all morning for both Carlene and me.

Janie's first question was, "Mom, did you mention the stranger our neighbor lady saw that night and how the jury would surely have decided differently if they had known about him? Also, did you tell them how you and Dad used to dance to the piped-in music at the grocery store?" I chuckled that only she would find the dancing amusing or interesting and that I remember a time when that embarrassed her.

When I arrived at the shop, my team member Rox asked if I told "those people" that she wouldn't have made it through the eighteen-month-long computer training if I hadn't subjected her to daily pep talks and tutoring. I smiled, "No, Roxie, I just mentioned that it was a very good program."

After dinner I called my parents. Mother asked, "Did you tell them how much we need you home and how much you've missed with your children all these years? Were they mean to you?"

"I'm sure they know how you feel, Momma, and no, they were not mean. In fact, they were very nice."

My daughter Sarah in Dallas inquired, "Did you tell them what a wonderful mother you are, and did you tell them about the person who was in the basement when we left the house that night?"

"No, Sade, I don't think we ever spoke about the flashlight in the basement."

I had also promised to call Helen Martin, who met with you last year. Helen spoke without taking a breath, "Did you talk about your life in prison and how violent that environment is, but even so you never have resorted to violence and would never be a threat to society?"

I gasped, "Oh, no, Helen, I told them about the time I threw a set of dishes at Bill!"

Helen scoffed, "That's not violence! You were just getting his attention. Did you tell them how super close you are to your family and how hard you work to mother your kids through the mail, the phone, and visits? Did you tell them that if released you'd be an asset to the community? I need to talk to them again! You left out all the important stuff!"

"Did they like you, Mom?" asked my youngest daughter Carrie.

"I don't know, but I did launch into my soapbox lecture about the importance of education in prison."

She moaned, "Oh, Mother, you didn't!"

Father Behan's big question was, "Did you discuss the plea agreements you were offered and how you'd already be home if you'd taken any one of them? To me that's the major issue here regardless of guilt or innocence. And, by the way, did my name come up?"

Last night at church, PATCH Board Vice-President Norma took me aside to ask, "How did the meeting go? Did you tell them how much you do for PATCH and how you helped write the PATCH parenting curriculum?"

"No," I answered, "In fact, when I told them about my prison work history, I completely forgot to mention that I left the law clerk job to be the PATCH clerk after Helen Martin paroled. I don't think I ever mentioned PATCH and how important the organization is."

When I found my sister home, she asked, "Did you tell them I have a room all ready for you and that you could do computer work for a living and not even leave the house if that's what they want and how much we need you to come home and how many people are rooting for you? People are always asking me when you're coming home." Mary was not pleased that I did not mention her room and computer.

I have tossed and turned every night since the meeting, thinking of all the points I should have made—especially after everyone so kindly pointed out my inadequacy. There is no one better than friends and family to let you know all the ways in which you have failed.

Mr. Bednar expressly requested that I write you with a good reason my sentence should be commuted. My guilt or innocence has nothing to do with the fact that I would be home right now if I had signed a plea agreement. No other lady in this prison has ever told me she was offered and refused a plea agreement on a capital crime such as the one of which I was charged. There is a lady who lives in my housing unit who shot and killed her husband as he slept. She accepted a plea agreement of fifteen years and will leave soon.

I place no blame on the judicial system. The prosecutor only did his job, and the jury did not have all the evidence on which to base their decision. I am not bitter. I have done every day of this prison term the best I can and make it my goal to accomplish as much as I can. I refuse to waste my life just because I'm not where I should be. If I had a quarter for every time someone in this prison had said, "Mrs. Prewitt, no matter what you did or didn't do to get in here, you sure don't belong here, and I hope you're doing something to get out."

My husband and I did not have our children without a sense of the enormous responsibility they imposed. I continue to guide my children and grandchildren and take care of their emotional needs as much as humanly possible from a distance. The overpowering love I have for my family cannot be diminished by razor-wire fences.

Lately, mail call is a mixture of anticipation and anguish for me. When my name is called, I look with dread for the official state envelope, which, in the past, has brought me the bad news of my denial for executive clemency.

Governor Carnahan, please commute my sentence. No public benefit is served by my continued incarceration, and I promise that if you decide mercifully, you will never once regret your decision.

December 22, 1997

Dear Gary,

Tonight at mail call, I received probably around twenty Christmas cards from dear friends and family, but none of them tickled me like your letter did. That was before I opened it, maybe because you are unknown to me, therefore, exciting. (I'm sure that makes no sense to you.)

I can tell that Mary gave you my address because you used "Patty

Ann"—only people who knew me in pigtails use both names.

This has been one of the most stressful weeks in my life. I'm too CRAZED to write a good letter. You know that Thursday Carlene and I met with the governor's representatives. Well, Mr. Bednar asked me a difficult question. He said, "If we don't believe in your innocence, why should the governor commute your sentence?"

I answered that if I had killed my dear husband, I deserved to stay right here—then started to cry. Joe told me to write my answer in a letter—so I've been working on that letter in my head and on paper since. Today I typed it up and mailed it. I sent Mary a copy. That was the hardest letter I've ever had to write. I kept praying for the words to convince them to free me. The responsibility is enormous! You can't imagine. My stomach is in knots.

Enough of that. It seems much of my life is consumed with the quest to be free.

I'm pleased as punch that you took time out of your busy schedule to answer my fan letter—since you have so many to go through. But I thought I had bad handwriting. Yours is horrible.

I never meant to make you cry with my letter. It was supposed to be funny! You're very tender—I could tell that by your songs. It just occurred to me that I'm writing away as if I knew you. All I really know is what I heard in your voice.

My sister looks at life through rose-colored glasses. She says you're wonderful, of course—and I'm sure she said the same about me. I won't believe her entirely if you don't. I'm sure she's told you that I'm beautiful—but I'm FAR from that. Don't let her lead you astray with her sweet talk.

I do like you, Mr. Kirkland. There is something very special about you. I'm sure your dog would agree.

You have a leg up on me. You know my family and gobs about me. I know very little about you. Where were you raised? I understand we are the same age. When's your birthday? Have you always been drawn to music?

This place is a zoo. We're supposed to pack up and leave January 5. I dread it with every fiber of my being. We will be strip searched, dressed in prison grays, shackled, chained, pushed into buses. Sigh.

I'm sure you don't want to hear about my nightmare life.

I'm glad you like my letter. I like to bring good feelings with my thirty-two cents. Thank you for answering me.

Just Let Things Unravel

Tuesday, January 6, 1998

Dearest Mary,

Yep, another address change. This time they've transported and deposited us on the far side of the state—about four hours from Kansas City on Highway 54. You can't miss us: the whole camp is made up of bright red, metal-sided buildings. Looks kinda like a strip mall in the Ozarks. Or a state mental institution. One of the staff referred to our new camp as "The Best Little Whorehouse in Vandalia."

Yesterday morning the big move began right after a hasty breakfast. The day before we had sorted and packed all our property in boxes and loaded trucks. Unfortunately, we had unseasoned custody staff who made a big torturous deal out of a simple transfer. I never heard so much hollering and barking and indecision and changes of plans.

It took forever, it seemed, to strip search, chain, and restrain us before we were allowed to hobble to the buses. Silently I kept repeating, "Breathe in, breathe out. Everything is as it should be." But the unruly and uncentered part of my mind was cursing like a sailor.

We rode before dawn, so I didn't get to rubberneck. It's been about five years since I've traveled. My stomach felt a bit queasy. Car sickness, I guess. Finally, as the sun began to peek over the flat farmland horizon, we saw a sign that read, "VANDALIA." I think the population is about 100. We rode into town to multiply that number by twenty.

As we each performed our leg-shackled leaps off the bus, hundreds of guards stood at attention as a show of force to deter us from any funny business. I had to smile to myself. We didn't want to rumble. We wanted to use the restroom and get a cup of coffee. Oh, and the smokers wanted to "burn one."

Our complete willingness to line up and get dechained and line up again to wait was a disappointment to the gung-ho guards. What did they expect, though? We're not men in a movie set in Alcatraz.

We're the first wave of inhabitants in this brand spanking new prison. We were herded into one housing unit. At first, I was completely lost, but finally figured out that the building is a central rotunda, a hub, where guards sit, and the housing units are like four spokes to the wheel, named simply A, B, C, and D.

The next phase of our day was spent recovering our personal property—the stuff we boxed up the day before. Loads of caseworkers and guards went through belongings to list it all and pitch anything they deemed unnecessary or not allowed. Utter chaos.

Helplessly I watched for hours while my friends lost all sorts of things that we can actually have by policy—like simple sewing kits. But none of the staff seemed to know the rules. By the time my turn came around, it was 6:30 in the evening, and I didn't give a big rat's ass what they took. I only wanted to lie down.

The caseworker and guard assigned to search my possessions must have felt the same way. The duo didn't confiscate a single item from me. Although they did discuss taking my summer sausage and eating it right then and there, that was the only close call.

Finally, I trudged down the strange hall to find my assigned cell and compare horror stories from the day with my three equally exhausted roomies. We four made our hard steel bunks with new, stiff, starched state sheets and fell into bed.

But a good night's sleep was not to be had. As Momma says,

"No rest for the weary." First of all, our sheets were noisy. Uncommonly loud. Whenever anyone moved even slightly, the crispy sheets crunched. The acoustics are horrible with cement-blocked walls, metal ceilings, and linoleum-tiled floors.

Also, none of the guards knew in which cell and bed we were assigned. They kept coming into the room rattling keys and asking where inmates were. Just as I'd drift off, another clank of keys and booming question.

This morning while we dressed for the day, Luz bemoaned something about "Prison Bingo." Luz is from Colombia in South America, so when she exclaimed, "I was so scared when the guards play Preez-own Bean-go last night," we didn't have a clue what she was talking about.

After much discussion, we realized that when a guard would barge into our room and say an inmate's name and one of us would tell him on which wing she lived or what room, it sounded like some sort of game to Luz. For example:

Guard: Parks
Answer: B
Guard: Jamerson
Answer: 104

It sounded like Prison Bingo to her, and she lay awake most of the night in fear that it would soon be her turn and she wouldn't have the correct answer. I know. It sounds crazy, but not if you know Luz.

The story of Luz is fascinating, although much of what she's told me has gone misunderstood because of her broken English and my lack of Spanish. As a teenager she found herself pregnant, so her strict Catholic father banished her from the family fold. After her son was born, she left him with her aunt, swam out to sea, and stowed away in a freighter. (I'm not making this up! What moxie! I wouldn't swim very far out in Lake Jacomo.)

Luz ended up in New York after escaping from slave status on an island where girls sew clothes for Americans. She then sent for her son and enrolled in college while working full time. An offer was made to drive a huge amount of cocaine across the country to California, and the money proved too tempting for the struggling single mother to refuse.

In Green County, just outside Springfield on the interstate, Luz was flagged. Imagine a beautiful Hispanic woman, wearing red lipstick and giant gold hoop earrings with long, luxurious, raven black hair, cruising through redneck country in a shiny new white Cadillac. Must have stood out like a ruby in a bed of river rock. Eighteen years is what she received, and she's served about six so far, but she's now petitioning for deportation.

Luz is amazing—wish you could meet her.

Our stark cell is fairly large—at least compared to what we've had thus far—and square. A barred window is directly across from the security-windowed door. Two steel bunks are bolted into place end-to-end on each of the side walls. Each bunk wears a thin green, plastic-covered mattress to hide the hard, unyielding steel. Pillows seemingly composed of large rocks camouflaged with blue stripe ticking come with each mattress.

Each bunk has a metal stand-up locker beside the head and a metal footlocker under it. The bunks, lockers, walls, and ceilings are all the same shade of off-white. The floor tiles are a mixture of colors: beige, slate blue, tan, and hospital-green, and set with no thought to pattern or design. (The same randomly laid tiles are found all through the whole institution.) We even have a little Formica-topped, metal-legged kitchen table in the middle of the cell surrounded by four hospital-green, molded-plastic chairs.

It just occurred to me that in every prison movie I've ever seen, the cell walls are plastered with photos, posters, pictures, etc. Well, none of those movies were set in Missouri. I've never lived in a prison where we were ever allowed to stick ANYTHING on the walls. We're not even allowed to set a greeting card on our locker. Bare walls are all you see here. We are allowed two picture frames, so that's how we personalize our areas. Those two frames full of photos and our own personal blankets mail ordered from Penney's, if you can afford one, make our bunk spaces distinct.

Each wing is two-story, and each floor has a bathroom fitted with four toilets and four sinks, a four-stall shower room, plus a small laundry room with a washer and dryer. The downstairs also contains a room full of mops, buckets, etc., with faucet and drain. Every prison I've ever been in has bucket rooms. The downstairs also boasts a dayroom with a TV and a tiny dishwashing sink sunk in a cute kitchen cabinet, a phone room with two collect-call-only wall phones, and a small "quiet" room for silent studiers.

Real mirrors have been hung above the lavatories, which is not good. Most of us have no idea how much we've aged. I've looked into hazy polished metal mirrors—kind of like car bumpers— for years.

The buildings are far apart and threaded together by narrow sidewalks on bare dirt grounds. No trees. No shrubbery. The spacious layout helps give the place its unwelcoming feel. We've been in some hellholes before, but at least those prisons had personality. This one lacks the haunted energy of past inhabitants. But it's clean!

Another shock is that we are required to wear our complete state gray uniform wherever we go. No exceptions. This ill-fitting outfit consists of gray polyester men's bell-bottom trousers and a matching button-down shirt. Men's clothes. And ugly battleship gray.

So far we're on lockdown status. The freshmen staff seem to be unnecessarily frightened that if allowed some fresh air, we'll immediately break away, race screaming like banshees, and hurl ourselves on or over the perimeter fence. I've never met more tense or serious people in my life.

They have a lot to learn about female convicts. Looks like we'll have plenty of time to teach them.

Tuesday, June 9, 1998

Dear Mary,

A girl who did a short bit at Old Renz in the early 90s has caught a new case and lives in my housing unit. Faith met me at breakfast this last week to catch up. You know how we girls are. Slowly we sauntered back to the housing unit still gabbing.

At the front door stood this sumo wrestler-looking guard. Although Faith was closer to him, he ignored her. I think her pregnant state put him off. She's large with child—almost due. He called me over to him to be pat searched. I hate that, but I did as I was told like a good little inmate.

He's so obese that his belly rubbed my backside. Yuck. He reached his short fat arms around me and with sweaty paws grabbed my breasts and squeezed so hard that it hurt. Horrified, I pushed his hands away, "Hey! Excuse me—you're not supposed to search like that. You're supposed to search me with the backs of your hands."

He grunted, stretched his arms back straight out, and grabbed my breasts yet again with a death grip. I pushed his beefy hands away a second time with the same admonishment.

I was smack in the middle of a female prisoner's nightmare. And he did it all over again for the third time! I was SICK.

Only Faith was witness to this sexual attack. The female officer, who was on the porch smoking, had her back to us as she told some long-winded story to an inmate who was totally engrossed. Faith stood frozen and helpless with her mouth wide open in shock.

The sumo wrestler finally figured he'd had enough—and the female guard was turning around, so he grunted, "You can go now."

I stumbled into the dorm feeling violated and ill—and my tender little breasts throbbed with pain! Bridget saw the look on my face and asked me what happened. As I told her, the sumo wrestler called me out to the rotunda. He needed my ID because he decided to write a conduct violation against me for disobeying a direct order.

When the sergeant read the violation to me, I stated, "I let him grope me not once, but three times. How was that disobeying?"

The alcoholic sergeant, who had already been drinking at 6 am, flatly advised, "Tell it to a caseworker."

I spoke to the FUM (functional unit manager) about the incident. She sympathized. When I spoke to my caseworker, he seemed to sympathize. But the female guard, who had not witnessed the incident, wrote a statement saying that I had refused to let the sumo wrestler touch me and had caused a big fuss. That was all they needed. Statements from me and Faith are worth nothing to them.

Since that pervert groped me, I've heard many stories about him. He sneaks into cells while girls are sleeping and fondles the helpless. He is a peeker, too. He likes to pull back shower curtains and peer into toilet stalls. Every girl I spoke to had some icky story to tell. Makes us shiver.

After we won our pat search suit in the late '80s, if an officer didn't abide by the consent decree rules, we could call attorney Paul Shy and get some help. But no more. This administration doesn't care about the rights of women. Judge Stephens, our knight in shining armor, has passed away. We can no longer choose the female officer to frisk us when one is available. But the guards are still supposed to search the breast area with the backs of their hands. That was one of the changes we brought about with our suit. But no one is here to monitor.

The inmate population has changed, too. This prison is mostly young girls who have no defense when a pervert is groping them. But the sexual dynamic gives them an upper hand when it comes to staff relationships. In other words, if a girl has been "friendly" with a guard, he'll more than likely cut her a great deal of slack when she needs it—when he's found her doing something she's not supposed to do.

We old gals who fought for equal rights in the free world and civil rights in prison in the '80s have mostly been paroled, and the few of us who are left because we can't get parole pick and choose our battles carefully. I recognize a losing battle when I see one.

I was found guilty of disobeying a direct order. The fat officer probably has his grubby hands on some other prisoner as I write this.

Life goes on. Life sentences go on. As my old cellie Theresa always said about prison, "Nothing changes but the changes."

Friday, June 12, 1998

Dear Marsha,

I'm in love. Yes, you read that right. I'm in love. Bet you never thought you'd get that message from me. Me either. I don't even know exactly what happened. Since you have no history concerning this phenomenon, let me start at the beginning—with my sister.

For several years Mary has periodically mentioned her musician friend—described as tall, good-looking, curly blonde hair and beard, nice, my age, and with a great sense of humor and amazing voice. I always let Mary's chatter on this subject go in one ear and out the other. First of all, what would a woman serving forever in prison do with a man—any man? Secondly, he's a musician. Everyone knows musicians are far from sane and stable.

To appease my well-meaning but sometimes irritating sister—in other words, to shut her up, I procured a Gary Kirkland cassette tape. He's recorded several albums. Although I hoped that his voice would grate on my nerves or just sound mediocre and I could end the discussion with Mary once and for all, I found his music not just appealing—his songs touched me very much, so much so that I was moved to write my very first fan letter. Momma always says, "Give people their roses while they live."

Just to make sure that this singer/yodeler wouldn't get the wrong idea, I made my bunkmate write one, too. Protection in numbers. Mary delivered the letters, and quite honestly, I figured that was the end of that.

But in turn my fan letter touched Gary, and he responded. He swears he was never a letter writer before, but I can't tell. He took to it like a duck to water. (This reference is to content, not to penmanship.)

Gary was an English major at William Jewell College and writes an excellent letter. This mail-male friendship became very special to me, I guess because he's intelligent, self-deprecating, witty, funny, kind, odd, sweet—and possesses this added indescribable ingredient that may have to do with the fact that he's originally from Georgia.

Gary sent me a photo of him standing beside a jackass. On the back, he scrawled, "I'm the one on the right."

After corresponding for several months, to my horror he mentioned the possibility of visiting. Since I couldn't come up with a valid excuse to deter him, I mailed a visitor application form. After I received notification of the approval, I kept that bit of information to myself.

By that time I had called him on the phone some, and during a conversation, he remarked, "Man! It sure takes them a long time to process those visiting forms. Shouldn't I be approved by now?"

I couldn't outright lie, so ineptly I admitted, "Oh, yeah, I guess I didn't tell you—you're approved. Good thing you mentioned that."

You know I'm not excessively shy and retiring, but the mere thought of meeting this man face-to-face caused great emotional fright! Not only have I not met a man in 100 years, but there was something special about this one that scared me—shook my world. I rued the day I penned that stupid fan letter.

April 2 arrived, the visit day. After I fixed myself up as best I could, I paced. Donna, one of my roomies, decided that curling my hair would help, so she heated up a curling iron and attempted to do something with my stick-straight long hair.

The agreed upon time of arrival came and went. "Maybe he's not coming. Maybe he decided to do something else. Where is he? Maybe he stood me up!" I couldn't decide if I wanted him to make it or not. More nervous pacing.

The rotunda officer put me out of my misery by announcing, "Prewitt, Patricia Prewitt. You have a visit." After the required strip search and change to the visiting uniform, I made my grand entrance. OK, Marsha, it was far from grand.

By the way, getting dressed turned out to be a prison ordeal. This happened to be like the very first day of the new visiting room uniforms. After I pulled on the tan high-water elastic-waist pants and tan hospital-like scrubs top, I looked down with horror. The vee neck was cut so low that I could not only see my bra, I could see the floor! "Officer, look! I can't wear this out there. I don't even know this man!"

The female guard agreed that the top was a bit too revealing, so she called in the male sergeant who stared. The pair stood stumped, so when I suggested that I wear my T-shirt under the big top, they decided that would work.

Big, 6'2" Gary stood uneasily in the middle of the nearly empty room dressed in old blue jeans and boots with a faded blue denim pearl-buttoned, cowboy shirt over a turquoise T-shirt. Bright blue plastic reading glasses hung from his neck and rested on his chest. Both his curly hair and beard could have used a trim. His blue eyes rested on me uncertainly. He looked SO cute.

We smiled and gave each other a brief, friendly hug. He was as stiff as a two-by-four. But with no time at all, we chatted and laughed like lifelong friends. Our apprehension melted into affinity. Amazingly, he was exactly the man of his letters.

No more than forty-five minutes into the visit, Gary announced, "I've been thinking...." I waited for a clue. "What if I got a room for the night and came back tomorrow?"

Before I even thought, my mouth opened in surprise and blurted, "Don't you have a life?"

Whether he did or not, he laughed heartily at my honesty, and did return the next day—and the next weekend. And practically every weekend since then. We have no sense. We've fallen desperately in love.

I could go on and on about Gary, but I'll spare you. Hey, you should hear Gary say "on and on" with his accent. He uses a very long o, like the word "owe," when he pronounces "on." I JUST LOVE IT! I HAVE lost my mind.

My folks have met Gary at one of their famous barn parties, but they couldn't put his name with his face. After all, many musicians have performed there through the years. When I first talked to my folks about Gary, my Daddy asked, "Is he a dandy?"

I laughed in answer, "Daddy, he's as far from a dandy as can be. In fact, he wears blue dime store reading glasses around his neck!"

So that is the story of how I fell in love. Love is not rational, but it sure is amazing!

Monday, November 30, 1998

Dear Nancy,

Gary's parents drove to the Midwest for Thanksgiving and stopped by here to meet me. I can't remember if I told you that Gary's Daddy is a minister. When Gary was young, his preacher Daddy decided to go back to school to further his education, so he packed up the family and brought his wife and four kids from Georgia to Missouri. That's how Gary and his siblings ended up north of the Mason-Dixon Line. Gary's Daddy has actually preached at Jimmy Carter's church in Plains on occasion!

Anyway, I arranged a special visit for the pair, and Gary escorted his mother and father in. I can only imagine how they felt to visit their middle son's "intended" in prison, but they graciously didn't let on.

The couple is so cute and so Southern. The soft, melodic accent is easy on the ears. Gary is going to look exactly like his father in twenty years. Gary's mother is an authentic Southern belle, and they both are full of humor—easy to meet and visit.

Later that evening at the motel, Gary's Daddy admitted a shock he experienced in the visiting room. While waiting outside to check in, he noticed a distinguished elderly white gentleman in line and thought, "Isn't it a shame he must visit his granddaughter in prison, poor man."

In the middle of our visit, Gary's Daddy happened to turn his head just in time to see a young Black woman bound across the room, grab that white-haired visitor in a bear hug, and plant a wet, very non-family-like kiss on his poised and puckered lips. Reverend Kirkland kept his surprise well hidden, but he couldn't wait to ask Gary about it.

Gary had to explain about sugar daddies. Sugar daddies are exactly what you think they are—and are a common prison phenomenon. Through personal ads, the internet, and by word of mouth, many female inmates find lonely men to write to and/or visit. These men are called "tricks" because they pay for services rendered. Except for an occasional broken heart, it's all fairly harmless.

I've known women who have extracted large sums of money with a good line and a friendly act. One of the most-used lines is, "A girl can get into a lot of trouble if she spends time in the TV room or the gym. It's dangerous in here, baby. But if I had my own color TV, I'd be able to stay safely on my bunk in my room." Cha-ching. $225. Amy used that line about ten times on ten different marks during her last bit.

Another is, "I'd really love to better myself, honey, and go to college, but I can't afford the tuition and book fees." Cha-ching. $175.

Years ago, a gal manipulated $1,500 from some poor slob, ostensibly for airfare to fly home to him. Turns out she had about eighteen more years to serve.

Those are the most extreme cases. More often, the trick shells out cigarette money for a little dirty talk or a nasty letter. Some of the men just want someone to talk to—someone to listen.

When my Daddy first noticed what was happening around him in the visiting room, he named it, "Dry prostitution." Momma is blithely unaware of this—and we're all glad.

Some sugar daddies are handed down from inmate to inmate—like T-shirts. These regulars smile and wave to me in the visiting area, because we've seen each other for years. This "hobby" keeps them active and out of trouble, I suppose. Whatever floats your boat.

In defense of the inmates who live off sugar daddies, prison wages are so low that with most jobs, a gal can't survive. We are provided toilet paper, sanitary napkins, and harsh state soap only, so to buy shampoo and the other basic hygiene needs, we must have money. How much can you buy for $7.50 a month?

Don't get me wrong. Not all the couples in the visiting room are using each other. Many loving couples work to retain the closeness of their relationship while they are separated by the distance of incarceration. Watching those couples has always caused me to smile and ache all at once—and now Gary and I are also in that difficult, but still joyous situation.

"All who joy would win must share it, for happiness was born a twin." —Lord Byron.

Many years ago I read that quote but didn't fully understand the meaning until now, after years alone before meeting Gary. I realize the sugar daddies have inherently known it all along.

Sometimes the visiting area can look like the Beetlejuice waiting room: strange people, strange events.

At Chillicothe in the late '80s, my friend Mary and I were visiting when a husband showed up and surprised his beautiful, raven-haired wife, who just happened to be cozied up with her boyfriend. Recognizing the husband, I whispered to Mary a brief explanation of what was happening, so we both watched expectantly. That's when I noticed that the two men could have been father and son. They were both tall, tan, long-haired blondes. Vikings. They reminded me of Vikings.

The younger boyfriend stood up, shook the older man's hand, and made a smooth, cool, and not-too-hasty retreat. The handsome husband eased into the still-warm seat next to Shirley and simply took over where the kid had left off. No argument. No confrontation. We expected some fireworks, but I guess it was not the first time. The inmate was a madam and doing time for promoting prostitution. Still, it was pretty entertaining.

April 14, 1999

Dearest Gary,

I fell into a trap tonight: the religion trap. How do I get sucked into these things?

A neighbor came to the door of my cell before the pre-noon count and asked if I had a Catholic Bible. Before I could answer, the obese Black woman in the room across the hall hollered, "Whadda fuck iza Catholic Bible?"

The quicksand shifted under my feet.

I really didn't want to get into the subject with her, but I couldn't just ignore her. She would only yell louder—and she has the lung power. I've always thought her talents were wasted selling drugs.

Eunice should be in the theater. She can PROJECT! And just like Glenn Close in that movie with Michael Douglas, she will NOT be ignored.

Knowing all that, with trepidation, I started my explanation, "Eunice, it's like a regular Bible, but there are added chapters—stories included that were not placed in the version...."

She cut me off, "Whaddya mean? King James WROTE da Bible. Er'boda know dat. He be DER! He be one ah da WISE MEN!! And King James din' leave out a muddafuckin' thin'."

How do you argue with that? Thankfully, I didn't have to. She ranted and raved to herself until count was called. We must be absolutely silent during count time. Sometimes that's a useful rule.

May 16, 1999

Dear Mary,

In prison one can tumble into trouble any minute of the day. No matter how hard we try, there's no way to prevent problems. Here's an example of a typical conversation:

"Ma'am, where did you get this pencil?"

"Ah, sir, I bought it at the canteen."

"Are you sure? You'd better think about that story. I'll ask again. Where did YOU get this pencil that I found in YOUR locker?"

"I really do believe—I mean, I KNOW I bought it at the canteen."

"They don't sell this brand. Now what do you have to say for yourself?"

"Ah, it's the brand the canteen sold back when I bought it."

"Do you have proof?"

Of course, no inmate has access to canteen purchase orders, so there is no way to prove what brand of pencil was sold at that time.

"I'm gonna let you off easy this time. Throw that pencil away, and I won't write a violation. OK?"

That same conversation can play out for a host of items including

120

toothpaste, crackers, paper, shower shoes, pens, plastic bowls—any item sold in the prison canteen. The only difference is that the verdict can change. Besides losing the item in question, we can also either receive what's known as "extra duty" or get a CDV.

Depending on how the guard feels at the particular moment, who you are, and if you appear properly chastised, he or she can give the inmate up to sixteen hours of extra duty—which usually means scrubbing toilets, floors, or whatever for a total of sixteen hours.

If the inmate receives a CDV, the caseworker can sentence her to anything from extra duty, a canteen spending limit, recreation or activity restriction, or hole time. And a CDV goes on our permanent prison record. As with the court system, there are no clearcut guidelines. In other words, it's a crap shoot.

The other night I thought I was in BIG, BIG trouble. While I perched on my bunk crocheting an afghan for Carrie and Tom, my name was announced over the loudspeaker. When I entered the rotunda, several stone-faced guards of a variety of ranks glared at me as if I'd stolen their donuts.

In a tenor voice that did not match his girth, the big one ordered me to the back. This was not good. I'm no mind reader, but I could tell they weren't inviting me to the privacy of the back room to say, "Hey, Prewitt, we ordered an extra banana split and wondered if you'd like to eat it."

As soon as we settled in chairs around the conference table, the big lieutenant grabbed a handful of papers and slammed them down on the table in front of me with such force that it sounded as if a gun had been fired in the room. He bellowed, "WHAT DO YOU KNOW ABOUT THESE?!"

My heart felt like it might just leap out of my chest—and I wouldn't have blamed it. I didn't want to be associated with me either right then. Also, I was only wearing my pj's and no undies. A woman feels a bit vulnerable in just her night clothes.

As my eyes quickly scanned the top page, the problem immediately came to me. The officers had evidently searched my desk at the shop. A few years ago I wrote a tracking system for prison investigators so they could keep an accounting of who did what when—for statistical reasons mostly.

Say the director of the Department of Corrections wants to know how many stabbings occurred in a specific prison during a specified year as compared to the previous year. Administrators are always asking for reports such as that to prove whether current policies are working or not.

My job was to write the software to allow the secretaries of investigators to both type in reports of incidents and generate printed reports. That system was my first assignment upon graduation, and I sweat blood over it. I'm pretty proud of the way it works, too. Not bad for a novice straight out of school.

I interviewed our own Renz investigators before I designed the screen and flow and was given a file folder of old "solved mysteries" to see how their department handles incidents. The names of the suspects, victims, and witnesses were blacked out for security reasons.

These very reports were sitting in front of me at that moment. Taking a deep breath while searching for a way to explain all this to the seemingly computer-illiterate panel of judges, I began my honest and earnest testimony.

When I finished with, "And that's why these reports were in my desk," the lieutenant leaned back and loudly declared, "NO SHIT!"

No shit? What did that mean? "No shit, no joke, you're going to the hole?" It was Friday night, and my boss Linda wouldn't be able to begin to spring me until Monday. OH NO! For a few moments my frightened heart quit trying to free itself in my chest and stopped altogether. No shit.

It's essential for hearts to beat, so both my heart and I were extremely thankful when the lieutenant slapped his hands on the table, and declared, "I had no idea that inmates did that kind of work! Hey, Ms. Prewitt, would you mind taking these papers back to work with you Monday to save me a trip?"

Was he kidding? "Of course, not, sir. I'll take care of that for you. No problem." No shit. Cooly, quickly, and thankfully I made my exit, clutching my paperwork to my chest.

That's how that particular lieutenant was christened with the nickname "No Shit" by the girls who work in our shop. When Donna told him what we called him, he simply reared back and let loose a high-pitched, good-natured laugh. No shit.

July 29, 1999

Dear Nancy,

I LOVE TORNADOES. I mean, I love the threat of tornadoes. Let me explain.

The rules concerning physical contact are very strict in the visiting room. At the beginning of a visit, Gary and I can hug once briefly and kiss once briefly—and I mean briefly, like a split second—and can repeat those two quick signs of affection at the very end, as he's heading out the door. We are allowed to hold hands, but our arms cannot touch in the process. It's all very unnatural and difficult for two people in love.

And in case you've ever heard of conjugal visits, you can be assured that Missouri would never, ever entertain the idea of such a concept. I understand that progressive states such as California allow overnight visits between husbands and wives, but Missouri is firmly in the Bible belt. Physical expressions of affection are considered sinful.

Next time you're out with your beau, Nancy, try not to touch him at all. You'll see how often you casually touch someone you care about. If his hair is windblown, you can't reach up and smooth it. If he has a piece of popcorn hitchhiking in his beard, you can't brush it off. If he offers you his arm as you walk, don't take it. Don't accidently touch clothed knees or shoes under the table. Ballerinas don't stay on their toes as much as we do.

Today while Gary was here, a lieutenant scurried in and breathlessly announced, "EVERYONE! ATTENTION! WE HAVE A TORNADO THAT TOUCHED DOWN JUST A FEW MILES FROM HERE! EVERYONE, GET TO A WALL AND AWAY FROM THE WINDOWS! NOW! THIS IS NOT A DRILL!"

Gary and I moved to an inside wall and squatted down as instructed. We had barely settled in, in fact Gary had yet to fully unfurl his long legs, when we were ordered to move farther away from the windows. So, we moved closer to the vending machines at the other side of the room. Again, we were attempting to get comfortable on the floor, when the same lieutenant changed her mind.

This time we found the perfect spot. Remember the counter that divides the vending machines from the seating area? Well, on the side of the counter near the drinking fountain, there's a knee hole. Usually, the inmate photographer uses that area as her desk.

It wasn't easy for big, tall Gary to climb in under there, but he made it. Easily I slipped in beside him under his strong arm and wrapped my arms around him. Our legs extended far out into the room, but the rest of us was cozy under the protection of the canopy of the Formica-covered particle board counter.

Nancy, we have never been allowed to cuddle like that. Feeling my body safely wrapped in Gary's tender yet firm embrace was heavenly. We held each other while guards ran helter skelter from door to window looking for the twister. With my head resting on his chest, I wanted time to stop, so I could just close my eyes and forever feel Gary's faithful and loyal heart thump steadily.

Ruby, the lieutenant, periodically stood at our feet, peered in, and spoke to us while wringing her hands. Sweet Ruby, who suffers ill health, was a new corrections officer when I first came to prison. She recently wrote a few lines to a country song about Gary and me to tease, because she is even more amazed than I that I'm in love.

Gary and I barely spoke. Breathing in time, we savored the unexpected, once-in-an-incarceration luxury of this physical manifestation of our love. Gary stroked my hair. It was just wonderful.

When a relieved guard burst into the room to announce that the threat of death and disaster was over, we reluctantly disengaged and crawled out of our safe haven and sat back at our table. Even then Gary and I remained uncharacteristically quiet. We tried to hold on to the warm feeling of physical closeness. I retained the rhythm of Gary's heartbeat in my head.

September 3, 1999

Dear Mary,

I hate to write bad stuff to you, but one of my friends is in a predicament. Since I've been in her sorry shoes, I feel so badly for her—but don't know what to do. I really hate to write this in case I'm called on the carpet about it. But I guess my need to unburden myself to you is stronger than my paranoia. I've buried this in the middle of this letter to try to keep it between you and me only.

My friend's supervisor, who's a COI, is making her life miserable, making very disgusting comments to her of a sexual nature. Well, at least that's how it began. Dirty jokes. It always begins with dirty jokes.

Then one day he was sitting across the room from where she sat. He ordered, "Spread your legs." My tall, brunette, and very pretty friend is slated to see the parole board in a couple of weeks. She's looking at a 2007 release if her hearing doesn't go well. If the guard causes her any trouble, her behavior report for the Board will look like she's a troublemaker. So she opened her legs for the sick bastard.

That would all be bad enough, but now he frisks her when she leaves her workstation—sometimes several times a day. He caresses her breasts and buttocks and between her legs. He's not searching. He's feeling her up. His slow, calculated groping is completely sexual in nature.

Of course, it's all carefully accomplished with no witnesses. He's done it before, I'm certain. The next step routinely is for him to order her to perform oral sex.

If she were to try to stop him, he'd "slam" her for "disobeying a direct order" and "creating a disturbance." That's immediate hole-time. She'd lose her job, her bed, and the perks we get for remaining violation-free. For example, she'd no longer be eligible to read her monthly book-on-tape to her granddaughter. (She's a very young granny. I just started to describe my friend to you, but thought better of it in case this letter is flagged.)

And worst of all, she'd go to her parole board hearing with a big, fat, awful violation to try to explain away. Most likely she will end

125

up spending more time in prison on this sentence if she refuses to go along with the pervert guard.

When my friend confided in me, the tears just hung in her big brown eyes until they grew so heavy that they were forced to roll down her sweet face. She's literally sick about it. But if she were to tell any staff person, she'd be handcuffed and placed in solitary confinement for investigation. We call it "cuffed and stuffed."

The investigation process can take months. For days, weeks, maybe months, she could be punished by cooling her heels in the hole. Disciplinary segregation in this camp is no joke. It's a mean place manned by even meaner people and rules. Most of us will do whatever it takes to stay away from that hellhole.

The investigator would eventually and invariably conclude that it all came down to her word against the perpetrator. The lying, cheating, law-breaking criminal's word against the word of a fine, upstanding, honest, taxpaying, married, respectable officer who's a grandpa, no less. Guess who would be believed? How do I know this scenario? I've seen it play out over and over through the years.

She's trying to change jobs. That's the only solution at this point. If she does find a new job and can convince her caseworker to let her change without revealing the real reason, that guard will only find another innocent victim to paw and terrorize. This is a part of prison life that few will discuss—our dirty little secret. If I say something, I'll end up in the hole for investigation with the same results—and take my friend down with me. The system is designed to protect the guilty.

Years ago at Renz I clerked for a man who literally chased me around the desk. Our superintendent caught wind of the situation and asked me what was going on—since he was looking for a good reason to get rid of that guy. I told him that IF something were happening, and IF I told, I knew that I would go to the hole while the stories were sorted out. He promised that I would reside down there for a relatively short time.

I only snorted. I wasn't about to be punished because the Department of Corrections is a pervert magnet. How did I resolve the situation? I told one of my sick supervisor's friends (another staff person) that I was going to call in my big little brother about it. Of course it was all a bluff, but it turned out to be a successful ploy. Not long after I dodged that bullet, the womanizer's non-stop drinking led to his dismissal.

Many of the men (and women) who work here do so just for the opportunity to sexually harass us. They love to work in the candy store. To them, we are of no actual value—just a big bunch of whores, and therefore fair game to talk to and treat in any way they want.

I receive little of the blatantly sexual treatment now because I've grown old, but I still see it going on all the time. If I had a dollar for every time I've been inappropriately touched for the so-called sake of security, I could buy myself outta here. We are blackmailed into allowing these "indiscretions" to occur because staff have all the power.

Think of the young girls, first-time offenders, who are hoping and praying to receive 120-day probation from their judges for minor crimes such as bad checks or marijuana possession. They've been warned that if they get so much as one CDV, they'll lose their chance to leave this prison within the 120-day period. Those kids are terrified and will do ANYTHING to prevent a write-up. Anything.

Unfortunately, these types of situations happen everywhere in the world. It's certainly NOT just a prison thing. The powerless are routinely victimized.

October 27, 1999

Dearest Gary,

As I exited the chow hall at noon, inadvertently I overheard a discussion between two young girls—ones who are obviously "meth heads"—emaciated, thin dull hair, sallow skin, rotten teeth. I understand meth is cooked from gnarly ingredients such as battery acid, Liquid Fire (a drain cleaner), ammonia, and cold pills.

No wonder their health and teeth suffer so. In the past few years, this place has become overrun with meth heads.

The taller one explained, "I KNEW I was sick. That stupid bitch of a nurse said nothing was wrong with me, but I finally saw the doctor. He could tell I was really sick."

The shorter one mumbled, "Hmmm," while cupping her tobacco-stained hands around the crimped, half-smoked and stubbed-out roll-your-own piece she gripped with her mouth in an ongoing struggle to light the short butt in the wind.

The taller one went on triumphantly, "He even told me what I have. The doctor said I have . . .," she slowed down to make sure of the pronunciation, "HI-PURR-KON-DREE-AH."

Is "hyperchondria" even worse than hypochondria?

Through the years I've heard all kinds of new words in prison. For example, have you ever heard the word "conversate?" Many prisoners use that word as a verb stolen from the noun "conversation." "All I be wanting ta do is jus' conversate wit you 'bout dis pro'lem. Hear me out. OK?" "We be cool—we be conversatin'—that be all."

The other day I heard, "When can we get to the gym? I be feenin' to work out. It's like a drug, ya know?" "Feenin'" comes from "fiending," which comes from "drug fiend." If you're feenin' for something, you want it badly, very badly.

"Trip" is another common prison word. It can be used as a synonym for the word fret. As in, "Don't trip on it, boo. It be workin' itself out." Or it can mean a person is not thinking clearly, "Man, I be trippin'." The word is nothing if not versatile.

If used as a noun—"Wow! That was a trip!"—it means that whatever happened was amazing or astounding or weird. Whatever it was, it wasn't normal. (I bet it derives from language surrounding the '60s "acid trip." ("Leave him alone—he's trippin', man.") A person can be a trip, also: "See that crazy ho o'er der? She's a trip." It's a trip.

"Fin-ta" is the way "fixin' to" is pronounced in prison. As a Southerner, you know well that fixin' to is the same as getting ready to. "Quit trippin', bitch! I was fin-ta bust her lip wide open and dot her eye."

The word "bitch" is now used in place of woman, female, lady. It's used to describe any woman—good ones, bad ones, any woman. "She be my bitch." "I be her bitch." "That thievin'-ass bitch stole my last cigarette." "Dat big-bootied bitch be so good ta me." It's a bitch!

When I first was locked up, I heard a woman call her enemy a "ho." I may not be the sharpest knife in the drawer, but it didn't take me long to figure out that ho is derived from whore. Puts a whole new meaning to the old farm saying, "She's as dull as a hoe."

It's almost chow time. It be nice conversating with ya', but I be feenin' for my state portion ah prison slop, and dey be fin-ta call chow. You be trippin' if you think I be missin' a meal!

Saturday, February 12, 2000

Dearest Gary,

Everyone keeps talking about how many women are locked up in the United States and why. Yesterday after you left and while waiting to undergo the end-of-visit strip search, I chatted with the really young, pretty, blonde girl next to me.

She's the one whose sweet husband brings their baby to see her every weekend. I mentioned to the girl how it does our hearts good to see him carefully tote in their daughter with the diaper bag, etc., and what a doting daddy he is.

She smiled ruefully and relayed, "Well, before I came to prison, he never so much as changed a diaper. He's the reason I'm here, and I wasn't planning to move back in with him when I get out. But I guess I'll have to. See, he gave me this case. But I leave in twelve days and a wake-up...."

The admission stunned me. Before I could pump her for more information, our turn came up. Later in our cell I mentioned to my roomies what she confessed to me. Mickie, a heroin addict and my resident expert on the criminal mind, suggested that he probably was dealing drugs, but when things got hot, he let her take the case. It evidently is a common occurrence for a man to allow, even force, a woman to do HIS time.

That's one reason there are so many women in prison. A bunch of men out there are cowardly, sniveling maggots who live off the kindness of blindly-in-love women. And a bunch of weak women out there stupidly go for the okey-doke. Can you tell this revelation does not sit right with me?

This also got me thinking about the thousands of women I've met in prison and why each came in. I cannot think of one case in which a man wasn't involved. My old-timers say that in the past, male lawbreakers never allowed criminal charges to be brought against their wives, mothers, or any female family member. The men felt protective of the mothers of their children. No matter what craziness the family was into, the family unit was still of great importance.

Unfortunately, I see a shift from the strong, stand-up male con to an impotent, irresponsible, self-serving version who no longer holds women up on a pedestal, no longer does his best to keep his children's mother home, no longer attempts to protect his offspring.

Is this change in attitude toward women and children country-wide? Is the number of deadbeat dads growing? What's going on?

Friday, May 5, 2000

Dearest Gary,

You're gonna love this little glimpse of prison conversation. Tonight, while I sat in a stall in the gym toilet, I overheard the following:

In a honey-coated coaxing tone, "Come on, baby, you be straight trippin'. Just gimme the troof. I can deal with wha'e'er ya tell me. Ya know I love ya no matta what. Come on, baby girl. You been messin' wit Peaches, ain't ya? I be knowin' all 'bout it, so jus' fess up so we can quit trippin' an' bein' all crazy an' shit." Then the honey was poured on so thick that I could hear it drip from each drawn-out syllable, "Come on, baaaabeeeeeee."

"Shit, boo. Yeah, I been wit Peaches...."

"WHAT!? I KNEW IT, YA LYING TREACHEROUS TRI-FLIN' HO! HOW COULDYA?!"

Her voice then cracked with a sob, and she moaned to the heavens, "Oh, Lordy, I wasted the best months of my life on this ugly no-good cheatin'-wit'-'erbody bitch."

MONTHS. I had to bite my lip to keep from laughing right out loud. Months.

That reminds me of another gym conversation. While setting up our steppers for aerobics, I overheard the young pudgy white girl behind me call someone a "fag." I don't appreciate name-calling. The girl must have noticed my expression as I turned to look at her, because she began, "Oh, Miss Patty, I'm no homosexual. I'm just 'gay for the stay.'"

That was the first time I heard it put that way. "Gay for the stay." But I'm still amazed that she could put down lesbians while playing like one. Strange way of looking at it, but pretty normal in prison.

Have you ever heard the word "bulldagger" out there? It's used in prison to describe someone who's engaged in homosexual activities. It can be used as a noun to describe the woman or a verb to describe what she does.

This is the way I hear it used all the time, "That ho over there started in bulldaggin' 'fore she got outta R&O." "Those fuckin' bulldaggers make me sick." "Can't even get into the fuckin' bathroom for all the fuckin' bulldaggers." "She ain't no bulldagger on the street." "Yeh, I be bulldaggin' some right now, but I don't be no homo for real!"

"Studbroad" is another prison term. If a woman affects the role of a male lover, she is described as a studbroad or stud for short. A stud dresses and acts as much like a man as possible. Studbroads are very popular—much sought after, fought over. I guess they're male substitutes in a manless world. It's very common to see studs living off their girlfriends in a gigolo way.

Here's an example of both new words used in a sentence: "Coco left six kids, came to prison, cut her hair all off, turned into a studbroad, and started bulldaggin'. Look, now, she has two white girls fightin' over her and keepin' her in canteen."

Now don't get me wrong, you know I have very good friends who are lesbians, boyish, and not just gay for the stay. They are gay for life. That's a whole different story. Not just a prison story, either.

September 30, 2000

Dearest Marsha,

Remember in school when something REALLY funny would occur, but we had to hold in our laughter—hang on and wait until later? Remember how difficult that was? Well, it happened to me, to the whole shop, today. Giggles just bubble out of my mouth whenever I think of Linda's sweet, shocked face. OK, I don't really giggle—I belly laugh.

The computer programming shop where I work is located in a corner room of the vocational education part of the building. Sometimes tours of citizens are brought through our area. Sometimes the tour stops to look at us. Sometimes they don't. Kinda like at the zoo when you can skip the Reptile House if you have no interest in lizards.

This afternoon I looked up from my terminal to spy a group of important-looking people heading straight for our door. It's my job to sound the warning, "Incoming!" To impress the importance of my announcement and describe the tour in one word, I added, "Suits!"

That got their attention. My fellow workers snapped to, but the funniest one was Linda, our supervisor. Linda is a cute, pretty, and petite young lady—around Janie's age—with curly dark hair and a fun-loving spirit. As soon as I hollered, she jumped up from her desk in her office and ran out into the main room with us.

I'm not really sure why she acted thusly—she could have stayed seated in her office. Maybe she wanted to appear busy. It's difficult to figure out why a person does what a person does in a state of panic. But she reached up for a potted plant that sat high on a metal cabinet.

Did I mention that Linda is a bit vertically challenged? Did I mention that the plants had been thoroughly watered that very morning? I just want you to get the whole picture.

Since Linda could barely reach the plant, she tipped it toward her to move it, and as soon as she did that, the excess water and loose soil spilled down her ample bosom. Yep, in the split second before the tour of dignitaries opened our door, Linda ruined the front of her crisp, clean white blouse. Also, in case you didn't know, water makes a white blouse invisible.

Since the incoming group was looking straight at me through the door's window, I had to smile welcomingly as if nothing were happening. Out of the corner of my eye, I could see Linda doing her best to find a place to hide so she could act as if she hadn't just dumped potting soil and dirty water down her front.

By the time the group entered our shop, Linda had positioned herself behind the lectern that I use for class. She's short enough that she did a pretty good job of hiding with her arms crossed over her chest in a valiant attempt to appear absolutely normal.

To distract the visitors, I smiled and presented my little dog and pony show—explaining and showing them what we do. Our work is really very interesting. We write tracking systems with menus and screens.

The other worker bees also talked to tour members about their work while doing wonderful jobs of keeping straight faces.

Linda remained glued to the podium and never let on—even when one of the tour ladies asked, "Are you teaching today?" Linda simply waved a hand while leaving her arm over the stain, "Oh no, not today."

As soon as the entourage was safely gone and out of the building, we all looked at our boss and burst into gales of laughter—even tears. The whole scene was like a Lucille Ball comedy segment, but we had to hold onto our laughter. That was PAINFUL!

Speaking of painful, did I tell you that the State of Missouri sued me for rent? Didn't think I was that rich or important, did you?

Inmates don't "shop" like real people. Once a week on our

scheduled day, we submit a list of the items we want then wait our turn. A wall and windows separate us from the stock. It makes sense. There are a few thieves here, ya know.

That canteen day when my name was called, the clerk leaned down, shoved her face out the window, and told me I had no money. "What? Of course I have money. It's payday!" The clerk insisted, so I walked across the camp to ask my caseworker.

She and I found out that my account was frozen, which means exactly what you think it means. The money was there, but I couldn't spend it. She also handed me a huge envelope loaded with legal papers. As I glanced over the packet, I realized that the attorney general of the State of Missouri had sued me for "cell fees." The AG's office wanted me to pay for the cost of my incarceration. The total was huge—thousands and thousands of dollars!

The way I see it, everyone can squirrel away a few bucks out of each paycheck. My kids might need some economic help, or I may need a retirement plan for when I parole in 2036. I'll be eighty-six and have paid no Social Security taxes, so I'll have no income. Longevity is in my genes. Just planning ahead. Or thought I was! The AG acted like I'd been sneaking my hard-earned state pay out to an illegal gambling ring!

Not knowing what to do, I called one of my trial attorneys, Phil, in a panic—since he's the only attorney I know. Although he's a criminal lawyer, he instructed me to send a copy of the AG's petition to him. Meanwhile, I couldn't even purchase a bar of Ivory soap.

To make a long, painful story short, Phil somehow convinced the AG that since this was an election year, it would appear pretty stupid for the state to spend thousands of dollars in legal fees to claim a poor prisoner's $400 that she earned for writing software for the state at slave wages compared to what real-life programmers make, thus saving the State of Missouri hundreds of thousands of tax dollars.

Phil might have mentioned how the story would appear in the newspapers too—but I wasn't privy to his methodology. However, he did it, and a few months later, I received notice from the AG's office that the suit had been dropped.

To make ends meet while my wages were on ice, I feverishly crocheted teddy bears and traded them in exchange for canteen. That particular method of earning a living is completely against the rules. There's no free enterprise allowed in the unfree side of the razor-wire fence, but a girl's gotta do what a girl's gotta do.

As soon as my account thawed and was liquid again, the teddy bear hustle ceased—much to the sorrow of eager customers. Inmate mothers are always on the hunt for gifts for their children and lovers are always looking for tokens of affection for girlfriends. But thankfully the factory is closed. I've resumed "legally" creating teddy bears only for loved ones or for charity.

October 17, 2000

Dear Helen,

I can't believe that Governor Carnahan, his son, and another man were killed in a plane crash last night. Dear God.

This morning, Carlene ran to me panicked and crying about what we're going to do now that he's gone. As you well know, we had been told that he promised to commute our sentences after the senate race next month.

But my first thought was for the Carnahan family. And Jean especially. She's become a widow. What a horrible tragedy. Are they sure it was mechanical problems with the plane? That's what the St. Louis news is reporting.

I can't keep from thinking about the Carnahan family and what they're experiencing. I've also lived through the devastation of losing both my beloved husband and son—barely lived through it. But Jean lost them both in the same awful accident. And her surviving children must feel like my children felt—heartbroken.

And I know you and Dale must feel shocked. You knew the governor personally. You and Dale sat with him in meetings! My daughter Jane and her sons met with him too—several times—and were impressed how sweet and personable he was. Everyone is aghast, in shock.

And in regard to our mission, first the pope threw a wrench in the works with his clemency appeal for that guy, Mease, on death row. When Governor Carnahan relented to the pope and traded Mease's death sentence for life with no parole, Carnahan took so much heat over that impromptu decision that he became clemency-shy and put us off. Now this calamity. Lord.

When I was first locked up, my very young nephew Jesse advised, "Aunt Patty, God has a plan—and when I figure it out, I'll let you know." I wonder if Jesse has any insights yet.

December 1, 2000

Dearest Gary,

You got me in trouble tonight! Well, it wasn't ALL your fault, but you had a hand in it.

I was talking to you on the phone when I realized no one was in the dayroom. "YIKES! IT MUST BE COUNT TIME!" I thought. There's no clock in that room, so it's easy to lose track of time. As soon as I hung up the phone, I attempted to slip invisibly back to my cell. Almost made it too. Almost.

"COME ON BACK HERE, MISSY!" bellowed the sergeant.

I stopped dead in my tracks and turned around with a wide-eyed, "Who, me?" expression.

The white shirt stood in the doorway of the rotunda glaring at me, "YOU KNOW IT'S COUNT TIME. WHERE ARE YOU SUPPOSED TO BE AT COUNT TIME?" As she lectured, she stepped into the dayroom and the door to the rotunda clicked shut behind her. We both froze.

The way the doors are designed, they can only be opened by the control panel in the rotunda or by keys. The rotunda was empty. I could tell by the panicked expression on her face that she did not have the keys. Oops.

She really went crazy on me then. Her face blew up big like a red balloon. This particular sergeant is a tall, big-boned woman with what I think of as "warrior breasts." You know the kind. They stand straight out like they're made of metal armor. Both breasts were pointing at me—accusing me of locking us in.

The sergeant and I heard two guards who had counted B wing pounding on the door. They were locked in as well. The sergeant stopped yelling at me and started yelling into the walkie-talkie—to no avail. She even ran clear up the stairs in a futile attempt to gain radio reception.

I perched on the sign-out table contemplating my fate. Either she was going to just pinch my head off right then and there during her tantrum, or I was surely going to the hole for "interfering with count" or, even worse, "escape attempt."

I heard the sergeant pounding on an upstairs window, trying to get the captain's attention. I ran to a downstairs window to do the same. The captain must have seen one of us, because she tossed her cigarette and marched across the camp to our housing unit. Once inside she found two blue shirts beating on the door of B wing, and the mad sergeant, her big breasts, and lil' ole me, locked in on A wing.

The captain reached to the control panel and popped the locks to allow the officers into the rotunda. I hopped back up on the sign-out desk hoping to sink into the furniture while I watched everyone excitedly explaining with flailing arms.

The captain was my COI while I was in R&O—when I first arrived at prison. The very day she came back here to work, she recognized me, "Mrs. Prewitt, I see you've stopped crying." My answer was that a person can only bawl so long. After all, it had been nearly fifteen years.

I kept staring at the captain's calm, reasonable countenance as the scarlet-faced sergeant ranted and raved. I prayed, too. You know those last-ditch prayers where you try to barter with the Almighty? "If you get me outta this one, Big Guy, I promise...."

Then a prison miracle occurred. The angelic captain leaned in the door and with a kind nod uttered the most wonderful eight words I've ever heard, "You can go back to your room now."

YES! Before the captain could blink, I raced back to my room and was whispering the lurid details of the close call to my concerned cellmates. YES! HALLELUJAH! This skinny prisoner will live to serve another day!

Next time I tell you that I MUST get off the phone, believe it!

February 9, 2001

Dear State Representative Merideth:

You are such a sweet person. Thank you so much for the nice note. It brought tears to my eyes. As you can imagine, I've felt pretty blue about the recent turn of events. We had worked so hard. Did you hear about what my poor children went through this weekend before the inauguration? If not, here's the scoop:

First of all, in December 1999 my oldest daughter Jane along with her two young sons met with Chief Counsel Joe Bednar at the capitol. Bednar asked if her father had any relatives, and Jane told him there were two sisters, her aunts, but that she'd had no contact with them for many years. Jane then offered to track them down and talk to them. Bednar assured her that it would be neither necessary nor prudent for her to do that, and that he would call the ladies if and when my sentence was commuted.

Then Saturday morning, less than two days prior to the inauguration, someone from the governor's office called my youngest daughter and asked for the whereabouts of her father's sisters. Poor Carrie barely remembers them and couldn't recall their names, but she and her sisters, who all live in Lee's Summit, put their heads together and found one of the aunts via the internet. When Jane called the capitol, she was told that one of the aunts had already been found and had replied: "Whatever is best for the kids and grandkids." The family was ecstatic.

But the rest of Saturday and most of Sunday was a roller coaster ride of emotions. Every phone call to or from the governor's office held a different story until Sunday evening when Jane was informed that there was opposition from their aunts and the prosecution, and that Governor Wilson had chosen to pass our clemency petition on to the next administration.

Now if I had accepted the plea agreement offered to me during the trial, I would have already been paroled. The prosecutor chose to ignore that fact and took the stance that if I dared serve one day less than fifty years, it would be a terrible travesty of justice.

Also, the now-grown children, who essentially lost both parents and have suffered from those losses every day for seventeen years, were not considered victims of the crime. Their voices were not to be heard. Their opinions mattered not.

That Sunday I sat in the concrete block phone room listening to my children sob as they told me what the governor's people put them through and how utterly helpless and very disappointed they felt. My already broken heart shattered into tiny pieces as I heard their cries.

That same weekend Johnson County prosecutor Mary Ann Young called the *Kansas City Star* requesting a story damning me and the governor's staff for even considering a reduction of my sentence. Jane called reporter Matt Campbell and asked why the children's side of the story was not sought. He had no explanation, but the *Star* promised Jane they'd print her rebuttal. They never did. Again, the children were not considered victims of the crime and were themselves victimized.

After that weekend a prison caseworker stopped me and commented, "So sorry about what they did to you this weekend. If you can't pass muster for a commutation, there's no hope for anyone else." Her kind remark only saddened me more, for Governor Wilson extended mercy to no one.

My father recently called Kansas City attorney Philip Cardarella, who told him that he'd met last year with Governor Carnahan, who pronounced that he would commute my sentence after the election. My hope is that Governor Holden will understand what Governor Carnahan planned and carry out his wishes in his name.

Do you have any ideas of what I or my supporters can do? We did everything we were told by Mr. Bednar for the last five years with no results.

You have no idea how much I appreciate your support and concern and especially kindness. My prison environment is far from benevolent, and so the goodness of nature you possess and take for granted is overwhelming to me. Thank you very, very much.

July 12, 2001

Dearest Gary,

Yesterday while standing in the dayroom waiting for the rec call—we can't go anywhere unless we are "released"—the loudspeaker squeaked, and instead of the expected, "INSIDE/OUTSIDE RECREATION," I heard, "PREWITT TO THE ROTUNDA."

When I pushed open the heavy steel and safety-glass door, the female officer ordered, "Have a seat right there."

"Rats!" I internally moaned as I settled into my appointed plastic chair. "This means I'll miss rec because it takes them forever to do UAs."

The officers work off a randomly picked computer-generated list, so urine analyses are done in groups. The rotunda was crowded with disgruntled women who had also been called to pee on demand. Looking around at the unhappy faces, I realized that a meeting of the newly formed we-had-other-plans-for-the-evening club had been called to order. Well, not exactly to order....

Laura, who's wheelchair bound, resides on another wing, so we commenced catching up about our children. Bragging, too. Others joined in until the sergeant firmly announced, "Ladies, there will be no conversation in my rotunda."

That shut us up, for a while. As other ladies came through the rotunda, conversing as they made their way to med pick up, rec, etc., Laura and I began to chat again. Others joined in until we again were admonished, "Didn't I just tell you that there will be NO talking in MY rotunda?" The sergeant gave us all a steely glance to punctuate his order. We fell into an uneasy silence.

Now, you'd think that we'd have learned our lesson by then, but oh, no. In a minute someone said something—then one responded—then another just had to interject her take on the subject—and before we knew it, this motley crew was chattering like chipmunks yet again.

The white shirt glared at our little society, hunched his shoulders, and hollered at the top of his lungs, "LADIES! I TOLD YOU! THERE WILL BE NO TALKING AT ALL IN MY ROTUNDA!"

Silence. We all looked appropriately chastised until I couldn't stop myself and softly advised, "Sir, where two or more women are gathered, unto each other they shall speak."

The sergeant stared at me, unblinking. Unblinking, I stared back, trying to read his mind. He must be a pretty good poker player. To lend credibility to my statement, I lied confidently, "It's in the Bible."

The sergeant blinked, then slowly swiveled his chair facing away from our sorority. The silence lasted a few beats until Tish felt compelled to comment on how long it was taking the female guard to process our paperwork. Of course, everyone joined in with an opinion.

July 31, 2001

Dear Nancy,

Here's a quick update on the ongoing quest for freedom. Senator Bill Kenney from Lee's Summit, who's a member of my brother's church, arranged for a meeting yesterday at the capitol for a group of my supporters. Daddy, Frank, Mary, pregnant Sarah, and Mary E. met with Chris Bauman, one of Governor Holden's attorneys.

You have good ole solid Jesse Ventura, but we have had three governors in the past six months!

Everyone reported to me that Chris was open and informed—a nice young man. He told the delegation that I have the biggest and most active clemency file in Missouri's history and maybe the best record of any prisoner in the state.

They did get the chance to explain a bit about Bill's sisters, who have come out of the woodwork to scream out against me ever paroling. And the assistant prosecutor, who is spreading untruths, was discussed. She denies that her office offered my defense team any plea agreements during the trial. You were there, Nancy, and I know better than that.

As Sarah said, if these people actually thought I was a crazed killer, how could they leave five little kids in my sole care alone in the country? Makes no sense. No one even anonymously called the child abuse hotline. That's because no one actually believed I killed Bill. It makes no sense that they have started hollering after all these years.

Did you know that when Bill's father passed away, the family did not inform my children? My girls think that the sisters (their aunts) feared they would have to share the estate, the inheritance. They didn't share. Guess they thought my poor college students would have no need for money.

It just occurred to me that maybe the sisters' fight to keep me in prison has nothing to do with revenge for their brother's death. Maybe they are afraid that if I were free, I would sue for Bill's share of the estate. Could it be that all this has to do with money?

I really had no idea that Bill's sisters and their families were so greedy and vengeful. They seemed like such nice people.

Anyway, the meeting went well. Everyone took the opportunity to put in their two cents. When Sarah asked what they could do right now to ensure success, Chris gave them two goals: 1) convince our legislative supporters to contact the governor with firmer political backing, and 2) secure job offers to prove employability and acceptance in the community. How to convince legislators to do anything eludes me, but the other mission is doable—and a pretty easy one considering my programming skills. But Lord knows I'd be happy as a clam to do ANY job in the free world. Give me a ditch to dig, a stall to muck out, a mountain of dishes to scrub. I'm ready and willing—and healthy as a horse!

It hurts my heart that my loved ones must endure these nerve-racking, heart-wrenching meetings—and have for so many years. They feel frustrated and so helpless. We all do.

September 3, 2001

Dearest Gary,

You should see the oval nearly-quarter-mile track absolutely FULL of females during six o'clock rec! Nice weather like this brings them out—and since we're so overcrowded, we have way too many women out there in the rec yard. Like ants at a picnic.

As I dodged, danced, and dove my way around the clusters of gossiping, slow-walking women in an attempt to get my speed up, I overheard two young girls discussing ways to escape. (Eavesdropping is known as "ear-hustling" in here.) I could tell neither girl had any inclination whatsoever to actually hop the fence, but that subject is pretty common among the confined. I'd wager that animals in the zoo talk about breaking out, too.

The little piece of conversation I caught reminded me of the actual escapes through which I've lived. When we were housed at Church Farm Renz next to the men, I noticed that some of them attempted to or did "decamp" monthly. Women rarely go to that extreme. Don't know if it's fear or family. Most of us wouldn't think of putting our families through that ordeal—and if we pulled it off, how would we see our kids?

The first escape I sat through occurred during my first incarcerated summer—1986. In those days we stood outside our cell door for count. We stood and stood that day until the officer finally put us in our cells and locked us in. Word that someone escaped filtered down our hall.

When a pullet flies the coop, the rest of the chickens are cooped up in the henhouse—for hours. We have no idea what's going on out there. Have guards on horses loosed the bloodhounds after giving them a sniff of the escapee's shirt? Are helicopters hovering?

Are the roads blocked? We never know. The remaining chickens are kept in an information vacuum.

During that particular lockdown, my cellie and I crocheted, shared our life stories, and listened to the rumble of our empty bellies. Years later when Lena, the escapee, returned to us, I informed her that we missed a good meal because of her. Don't think she cared.

I just remembered the prison lesson my cellie taught me while we were on lockdown: How to "wash stamps." In those days, prisoners recycled postage stamps. The used stamps were soaked in shampoo water. The envelope separated from the stamp AND the federal stamp ink washed away, too. Then the rejuvenated stamps were carefully dried and glued on envelopes with toothpaste. Toothpaste was the glue of the time. It not only worked, but your mail also smelled minty fresh.

Helen collects stamps, so when I spy an interesting design, I tear it off the envelope for her. An officer, who was tossing my cell, had a cow over my little stash of used stamps. Stamp collecting was a foreign hobby to her. Stamp washing was not. To appease the guard, I put the stamps in an envelope and mailed them right in front of her eyes to prove that I did not plan to cheat the government out of a couple of bucks.

The next escape was on the coldest day of the year right after Christmas in 1990. Two enterprising women picked the lock of my office in the Education Department, on a weekend day, and removed the glass of a then-unbarred window to slip out—right behind my computer terminal. When the state trooper spotted two shivering women, one white and one Black, attempting to hitch a ride along the highway in the country, he pulled over to either help or investigate. Rumor has it that Thelma practically jumped into his arms because she was freezing. I bet tougher Rena was not so happy.

In early March 1991, during the evening count, I heard the guard mumbling under his breath and looked around to see who was missing. As soon as I spied Lisa's empty top bunk and then the furtive look on her bunkmate's face, I knew young Lisa had made her getaway.

When the teenager first arrived at Renz, she earned her GED in the department where I worked. My heart always went out to her, because a group of young people were involved in a murder, and they all rolled on each other (snitched for deals)—except Lisa, who received the big time: life with no parole.

Lisa had no time or opportunity to live a real life in the free world. With no children to think about, her never-ending time wore on her, like an ill-fitting pair of shoes rubs a blister on your heel. So, she did something about it. She and another girl cut the already weak fence behind the gym and left. A getaway ride was waiting for them, then they split up quickly. The alcoholic accomplice was nabbed months later, but Lisa remained free for about five years. Most inmates and staff, secretly, wished her well.

America's Most Wanted came through, and Lisa, who by that time was a law-abiding, doting mother in a stable relationship, was nabbed. She spent years in the hole at Chillicothe and rarely sees her daughter now. The whole story saddens me.

Right after the Flood of '93 when we were given the work-release prison behind Church Farm, two unfettered girls who worked in food service storage saw a way to skip out and went for it. Unfortunately, their plan was flawed, because they ended up at a grocery store a few miles away and were immediately spotted by one of our guards who had stopped for smokes and donuts for the day. Darn the luck. Jennifer, who by the way is Lisa's fall partner (caught the case with her) and is serving a regular life sentence, and Vicky quickly were returned and sent to the hole to await prosecution.

In July of '97, word of a mini escape attempt traveled to us at Renz. Two impulsive females pushed out the window air conditioning unit in their cell at Chillicothe and crawled out the hole, only to have officers ride down on them right that minute before their feet hit the ground and before the duo could even think about getting to the fence. Seems that an enemy inmate had ear-hustled and snitched them out.

In Missouri, escapes are worth five years. Flat. Prisoners use the term "flat" to describe time that will be done day for day with no chance of parole before the days are done. My sentence is a flat sentence. Fifty flat.

All these girls were prosecuted and given an extra five-year sentence tacked on at the end of their time. No one ever told me if it was worth it or not, but I bet if I asked Lisa, she'd say her years of freedom and the birth of her little girl are a gift she gave herself.

December 12, 2001

Dear Mary,

"Old head" lifers, such as me, are called upon whenever anyone needs anything, staff or inmate: information, advice, canteen, addresses, how to spell a word, someone to take care of her baby until she paroles—anything. We are used as parole analysts, educators, suppliers, lobbyists, typists, mediators, confidants, advocates, problem-solvers, tutors, mommas, counselors, legal advisors. But if we don't come through, we turn into "life-doin'-bitches" at the drop of a hat. For example:

"Hey Miss Patty, gimme a soup and a soda?" If I don't, the next remark is more like, "Ya life-doin' never-goin'-home gonna-die-in-this-muddafuckin'-prison dirty-triflin'-bitches are all the same." We grow thick skins in here.

Oh, by the way "a soup" is a cheap ramen noodle soup package. Prisoners live on them. I know girls who eat dry noodles uncooked as a snack! But a little hot water in a plastic cup will usually bring the noodles to life. There are creative ways to fix them, too. They can become a dessert or a main dish. If you'd like any recipes just let me know. I personally don't eat them—the smell makes me sick. Too many years of smelling a dorm full of the sodium-heavy aroma of ramen soups, I guess.

Back to my story. Being a life-doin'-bitch is sad, but the recidivists are even sadder. "Recidivist" is a Department of Corrections term for a repeat offender—one who can't stay out of prison. It's said that these people are doing "life on the installment plan." My dear pal Mickie is a prime example.

Mickie has been in and out of prison for more than two decades. In fact, since I've known her, she's been "in" more than "out." She catches stealing cases (shoplifting is known as boosting), but her heroin addiction is the real culprit. And the saddest part is that she freely admits that life is better for her IN prison.

Her incarcerated life is organized, orderly, safe, peaceful. She bears no responsibilities—we are told when to get up, when to eat, when to go to the canteen, when to go to bed, when to use the bathroom. These aspects of prison that I detest are her salvation. In the free world, Mickie has no peace, no structure, no control.

As much as she complains about the guards, the rules, the food, the insanity, this is a better home to her than she's ever found in the free world. And she makes sure she spends as much of her life safely behind bars as possible.

That reality is sadder than the fact that I am a life-doin'-bitch who can't find my way back home. I embrace my responsibilities. I do not hide from them. No matter where I am, I choose to find peace and joy. No matter where Mickie is, she can't.

Mickie, who's good-looking, a wonderfully loyal friend, and sharp as a tack, comes from a family of criminals—she was sexually molested when she was young. Life has been no bed of roses. Drugs numb the pain. Stealing pays for the drugs. Her sons are all drug addicts in and out of prison, too. As Hank Williams, Jr. sings, "It's a family tradition."

Mick calls me "Bubble Girl," because, according to her, I was raised in a strange world where people are truthful and open, mommas and daddies love their children and each other, uncles would never ever dream of taking sexual liberties with nieces or nephews, everyone works honestly and diligently, and no one breaks the law. The bubble in which I grew up is a bubble full of love and joy and trust—a bubble that people like Mickie can't even imagine.

When Mickie is free, she self-medicates with any kind of drug available. When she's in prison, she lets the state dull the emotional pain with psych drugs. So even in "stir," she doesn't FEEL, and she doesn't DEAL. Mick won't step back and take a hard look at herself—why she does what she does—and make a change.

Is it laziness or fear? Both. In my opinion, both are factors. As a life-doin'-bitch, I've had plenty of time to conduct my own scientific observation. I see the same women caught in the revolving door of recidivism. These are women who can't or won't grab control of their lives.

And my heart goes out to them. I desperately want them to stop and see what they are doing. These are good women who could make great contributions and live good lives. They have children and grandchildren who need them. Sleeping, the long-medicated slumber of depressed inmates, is a waste of their precious lives. And life is precious.

Well, I have described the problem, so where is my solution? That, I don't know. I want to slap these good women, like Cher slapped Nicolas Cage in *Moonstruck*, "SNAP OUT OF IT!" There must be a way to get through to them.

But prison only compounds the problem, cripples the already lame, lowers their already diminished sense of self-worth, hands them even more excuses for failure. Prison is not the answer. These women need help and support when they are in the free world. They need assistance when life becomes overwhelming. Obviously, they can't manage on their own. Help! They need help!

That's my hope—that good citizens pick these ladies up when they falter, so they can find their place in the world and stay out of this hellhole, that the state ceases its blind willingness to incarcerate these women and looks for alternatives to prison.

And I hope that my recidivist sisters-by-incarceration reach out for help—and not give up so easily. Please, friends, do not escape from life—and bury your heads under gray state wool blankets in the false security of cold, steel prison bunks.

But nobody wants that kind of advice from a life-doin'-bitch. How do I know? Because I freely offer it to recidivist friends who only roll their eyes, roll over on their bunks, cover their heads, and go back to sleep.

Thursday, January 31, 2002

Dearest Gary,

Wanna hear about our prison week so far? The digital clocks historically sold in the canteen also have radios. These appliances are now considered contraband. The new clocks currently sold in the canteen are just digital clocks without the radio. So, if you don't want a contraband violation, you have to dispose of your clock radio and buy the new clocks. Makes no sense? That's the point.

Of course, ALL the clocks we are speaking of were or are sold in the prison canteen. We buy things, then are told to get rid of these things and buy other things that are suspiciously like the things we had to discard. This happens all the time.

Powders, like Shower to Shower, are contraband, but baby powder is not. Colored pencils bought in the canteen are now contraband, but colored pencils bought through a craft order are not. They are the same pencils. But not the same in the eyes of the powers-that-be.

Some of these items are still being sold at the canteen on the very day they are considered contraband. One woman told me she bought a headphone extension on Monday and had to discard it on Wednesday. Yep.

Rumor has it that we will soon have to send out all our red or blue clothing because they are gang-related colors. I'm sitting here in a red cotton turtleneck pullover. You know the kind. All middle-aged women have one. It's a classic style, comfortable, wears well, serves for a host of occasions—and I guarantee I do not look like any kind of gang member, unless we're referring to the over-the-hill gang.

But if the scuttlebutt is true, I will be forced to get rid of this and pay for a new one in a less dangerous color—like green. But is Greenpeace considered a gang? What color is safe? If you wear pink or baby blue, could it mean you've pledged a gang but aren't a full member yet? Does purple mean you're straddling the fence?

In the mid '90s, we had to send out all our black clothing because it was feared we would dress in black and pass for an officer. Even black yarn became contraband just in case we decided to crochet up a uniform. See, the E-Squad (Emergency Response Team), aka the goon squad, wears all black when they kick in on us for a shakedown. Around that same period of time, we had to get rid of denim trousers and shorts. I never was given a good reason for that one. We can still possess denim shirts and jackets—just no denim below the waist.

I remember in 1990 when we could still wear jeans, but the rule was the jeans had to be dark indigo, not stonewashed, not acid-washed, no colors. The policy stated "blue jeans" and that was taken quite literally. It took some tall talking to explain that my indigo jeans could not sustain the dark color through repeated washings. An officer accused me of having a pair of the dreaded contraband stonewashed jeans, when in truth, the poor Levi's had started life dark blue and naturally faded to the soft blue that denim lovers favor.

I have spent a small fortune (remember that fortunes are relative) on items that were legal, only to find out they have been declared illegal. I have bought scissors, mirrors, tweezers, toenail clippers, extension cords, stingers, crockpots, art and craft supplies, crochet hooks, reading lamps, clocks, oatmeal and honey facial scrub, key rings, dental floss, etc., in good faith only to find out that I was holding contraband and could get in big trouble! Having purchased items through the proper channels is no defense in prison.

Most people think of prison contraband in terms of weapons or drugs. They think of homemade knives, guns, and other harmful things. In our prison, contraband can be an extra pair of panties. We are allowed only seven. Guards frisk us in search of Chapstick or candy. Those items are contraband if found in a pocket.

I could write a book about prison contraband and never once mention a shank or tattoo gun—mainly because I've never seen either in person, only in movies. Come to think of it, I've never seen a prison movie where the convict was told that his oatmeal and honey facial scrub had better be disposed of—or else.

Yesterday certain hours were set aside for us hapless inmates to go to the Property Department to dispose of our contraband. A huge line of law-abiding ladies clutching body powder, digital clocks, colored pencils, and other questionable, although canteen-purchased, items, quickly assembled. An officer ordered everyone to go back to the housing unit except five, "There can only be five in the line at one time."

So, the mob dispersed and trudged back to the dorm. Once inside the dorm, this announcement was heard over the loudspeaker, "ANYONE WANTING TO SEND OUT CONTRABAND IS TO REPORT TO PROPERTY NOW!" So everyone gathered up their odds and ends and headed back to Property.

Once we reassembled, the officers once again advised us of the five-in-the-line rule, so grudgingly we trudged back to our quarters still in possession of the newly deemed contraband—only upon arrival to hear, "LAST CHANCE TO SEND OUT CONTRABAND. REPORT TO PROPERTY NOW." You think I'm making this up, don't you? My imagination is not creative enough to come up with this stuff.

Now handmade items are also problems. We are, by policy, allowed one completed craft item and one in-progress craft item. In other words, I can have my completed afghan plus I can have one project on which I currently work. But as soon as I finish the last stitch on a crocheted teddy bear and clip the yarn, the bear changes from "in progress" to "completed" in a split second. Bam! Just that quickly I am in possession of one more completed craft item than I am allowed! One minute, I'm lawful. The next minute, I'm just begging for a contraband violation! Do you see the stress in which we crafty gals live under? Enormous.

When we first arrived here at Vandalia, cigarette lighters were contraband. Of course, no one is supposed to smoke in the buildings, so when smoke breaks were called, right outside the door, the women had to get lights from the officers. Cheap in-wall lighters were installed on the siding of the building, but they broke almost immediately.

Smokers, as with all addicts, are ingenious and driven. The girls were actually undoing and somehow rigging electrical outlets to light their cigarettes. Scary! Those with the proper skills traded sexual favors for lighters. The administration considered their options and relented. The girls can now have lighters that are sold in the canteen. Still, no one by law was permitted to smoke in the buildings, but all the smokers do. There is no way to stop them!

Not only are certain items contraband, where we set our stuff can make the stuff contraband. For instance, if I place my Bible on my locker, the Good Book becomes contraband. An innocent wet towel turns into contraband if draped over the locker door to dry. We are constantly on guard for infractions that so naturally occur when a person inhabits a space.

For example, the inclination to set a beverage, such as a plastic cup of coffee, and a bowl of chips on the locker at the head of the bunk while reading a book is only natural. But if we let our guard down, we can be in violation of the housing unit rules: "Two picture frames, one radio, and one locker scarf ONLY allowed on top of the standing locker." Sigh—your tax dollars at work.

February 20, 2002

Dear Representative Charles Q. Troupe:

A few minutes after 11 pm on Saturday, February 16, 2002, I woke up to Mickie shaking my shoulder and whispering, "Patty, wake up. I'm bleeding bad and need to go to medical." I leapt out of bed in a hurry. In all the years I've known Mickie, she has never woken me in the middle of the night for any reason. A little more than two weeks ago Mickie had undergone major surgery—hysterectomy and appendectomy. She should not be bleeding.

As I pulled on my state gray pants, Mickie explained in a shaky whisper that she was experiencing great pain and when she went to the bathroom, a gust of bright red blood and clots filled the toilet. She put on three sanitary napkins and tried to get back to the room, but she filled the three pads immediately.

Feeling sick and weak and faint, she changed her pads again and made her way to the rotunda where the officers sit. She explained to them what was occurring, and although the 11:15 count had not commenced, she was instructed that she must wait for count to be taken and cleared before she could go to medical.

She sat in her bunk all bent over, barely speaking, "Ask the officer if I have to change to grays." Petrified, I rushed out to the hall where the officer was now counting. When I asked Mickie's question, he answered, "Of course." I mumbled, "Guess the uniform is more important than someone's life."

I still remember when my friend died in her bunk at Renz while we were trying to pull her state gray uniform on her. "Can't go out anywhere without the grays no matter what" was their mindset then, too.

After I helped Mickie get dressed properly, I rushed up to the rotunda to get the rickety housing unit wheelchair for transportation. Why I rushed, I have no idea, because once we were in the rotunda ready to leave for medical, the female officer stated, "No one is going anywhere until count clears." So, I stood there helplessly behind the wheelchair and watched Mickie doubled over in pain while she bled. I stood there for over forty-five minutes—sick at heart and praying.

The phone rang. It was a nurse asking for the bloody sanitaries. Evidently, she thought we had just decided to create some drama in the middle of the night. No matter that neither of us had ever done anything like this in all our years in prison. No matter that the officers could see how badly Mickie looked or that one of the officers had actually seen the toilet full of blood. Inmates are all liars and con artists.

I stomped off to the communal bathroom and rummaged through the trash. The male officer showed up behind me with a trash bag. Turning to him I stated in frustration, "There are over fifty pads in this trash, and I don't have the slightest idea which ones are Mickie's." With that I scrubbed my hands at the sink and marched past him back to the bubble. Furious is a place I rarely go, but they had put me there.

Somehow it was finally deemed acceptable for us to wheel to medical, but when we arrived there, we were met with more glances of contempt and derision instead of the assistance for which I prayed. A nurse took Mickie's blood pressure sitting, standing, and prone.

She phoned the pediatrician on call, and we were sent back to the dorm. The diagnosis seemed to be that this was perfectly normal. Mickie was given a pill for pain, only after she asked plaintively, and was told to come back in the morning to leave a blood sample, which we did.

Not one of the medical personnel actually examined Mickie. I won't even go into the excruciating experience involved in extracting her blood sample. I'll simply mention that even the officer on duty had to turn his head as the nurse dug around in Mickie's arm searching for a vein.

Yesterday, Gary called Central Office and spoke with Bryan Goeke about Mick. Gary didn't know what else to do. So yesterday morning, Ms. Pearl, our housing unit FUM, called Mickie back to her office to tell her that Superintendent Cornell had investigated Mickie's health issue and was satisfied that she was receiving proper care. Pearl told Mickie that she was being "monitored," and that excessive bleeding and pain was perfectly normal a couple of weeks after major surgery. Mickie observed that unless there's a camera above her bunk, no one was monitoring the situation.

This morning before I left for work, the officer ordered Mickie out of bed, along with a herd of ladies, for a urine drop. As Mickie pulled on her shoes to go to the dayroom to sit and wait to be strip searched and the sample given, I stated to her, "I guess this is what they mean by monitored." She smiled weakly.

Wednesday, February 20, 2002

Dearest Gary,

Remember all the fervor over the digital clocks versus the digital clocks? Well, today the associate superintendent actually issued a memo permitting us to keep the original electric digital clocks. She gave us the go-ahead to keep clocks that we have already given up.

In effect, she ordered, "Get rid of the clocks." Then after they were gone, she relented, "Ah, go ahead and keep them." Keep them how? They are no longer in our possession. You can't keep what you don't have anymore. Is it just me? Or is this insanity? My friends and I could do nothing but shake our heads.

Things have gone downhill since the Department of Corrections started calling us "offenders." Honest. When I first came to prison in '86, the DOC referred to us as either "inmates" or "residents." Then a few years ago, legislation was passed to change our collective name to "offenders."

My shop was required to change all the hardcoding on department printed reports, screens, and computer programs. Department stationery was updated. The letterhead stationery and forms with the word "INMATE" printed on it was pitched, wasted, to make room for the new improved paper products with "OFFENDER."

We noticed that as soon as we became known as offenders, we received even less respect. But it only makes sense. Maybe a rose by any other name would smell as sweet, but a person called "honey" is treated differently than one called "stinky." It's only human nature.

My kids just HATE to see that word on my prison ID. Janie said the word offends HER! Offenders are those who have offended. People who offend, whether it's a matter of body odor or worse, are shunned like the lepers of old. It matters not if a prison offender is a lovely lady with a sunny disposition who wouldn't hurt a fly. She's still offensive in the eyes of the law and the Department of Corrections.

But if this department is set up to "correct," as claimed, shouldn't the correction happen for the good? If a barn is leaning, and someone corrects it, we assume it no longer leans, that it's straight. Follow me? If a person is corrected by the whole department set up to correct, shouldn't she be better after the correction than before?

How can she actually be any bit better if she's treated as if she were worse? That's the rub. It's a conundrum. Prison is actually the Department of Anti-Corrections. No one leaves here standing straight and tall, feeling better about herself.

All the friends I've sent out into the world over all these years felt the same way: overwhelmed, frightened, and not as good as free people—ashamed. One of my friends told me that as she scurried down the street in Kansas City hunting for her first after-prison job, she felt like she had a stamp on her forehead that read, "CONVICT! BEWARE!"

We who are in prison are treated poorly because we are "offensive." The ladies who leave prison must overcome much prejudice in the free world because they will always be considered "offensive." Every one of my paroled sisters-by-incarceration has my admiration and prayers—and I want so much to someday be counted among them!

June 31, 2002

Dearest Momma and Daddy,

Can you believe your oldest daughter is turning fifty-three in a few days? I feel like I'm still thirteen too. How does that happen? And Morgan, who not long ago was called Little Bunky, just turned twenty-five! Where did that quarter century go?

Remember when Mickie had a hysterectomy in February and started bleeding and hurting really bad right after that? Scared me to death. Well, she finally found out what's going on. She saw a state doctor yesterday who actually examined her. Yep. No doctor up until then actually LOOKED at her. After poking around the doctor proclaimed that she tore some of her internal stitches not long after surgery. That accounts for the pain. The blood was from the tear, too. It's just a good thing she didn't rip out the embroidery too much. Are they going to do anything about it? Of course not. She hasn't died yet!

Mickie thinks it happened when she attempted to get out of the sedan while in shackles and chains. You know how difficult it is to pull yourself out of a back seat normally? Just imagine wearing a belly chain and handcuffs plus leg shackles. Mick had no way to use her hands. She felt a sharp pain while straining to exit the cop car.

We do feel better now that a doctor has at least evaluated the condition and there's a logical answer to the mystery. She still bleeds, but much less. Don't fret about it. Mick's getting better every day.

Nothin' Changes But the Changes

July 12, 2002

Dear Nancy,

When I see hungry women, it bothers me. I know exactly what it feels like to try to fall asleep when my empty stomach is demanding attention. I've filled up with water to stop the ache—only to have to keep getting up all night to pee. Fortunately, right now I work at a great paying job writing software, but I have in the past scraped by on $7.50 per month base pay. That makes for "hard time."

For hygiene care, the state provides only bars of harsh lye soap manufactured by male prisoners. So, we inmates must purchase shampoo, lotion, laundry detergent, deodorant, toothpaste, toothbrushes, and any other hygiene items we need. The canteen prices are retail plus 20 percent markup. The 20 percent goes into a canteen fund used to purchase all the books in the law, recreation, and chapel libraries, all supplies for the GED students, all the recreation supplies, all the appliances on the housing units (washers, dryers, etc.), and a host of other stuff.

The bottom line is that many of the inmates here are extremely poor. The rich rarely come to prison. Just ask O. J. These poverty-stricken girls are hungry. The state portion of gruel is rarely enough. Supper is around 5 pm. Breakfast is never before 5:45

am. Those twelve-plus hours can be very long. Yesterday during lunch, as I rose to leave the table, a little girl with light brown hair and dull gray eyes, who I'd never seen before, called to me, "Hey, ma'am, are you gonna eat your stew and bread?"

We are served two pieces of white bread at every meal, and I never eat them, so giving my bread away is normal. I responded, "Of course, you can have the bread, but I ate half of the stew...."

As she eagerly scooped the fat, gristle, and other stew remains from my tray to hers, she responded, "That's OK. You look clean."

I almost laughed, but honestly the whole exchange was sad to me. These girls are so poor they'll eat food that is laced with another's saliva—and they fish cigarette butts out of ashcans. They play Russian roulette with their health to get their bellies full and a nicotine fix. Don't they know that most of our population has Hep C, HIV, herpes, TB, staph, or some other horrible communicable disease, not to mention the common cold and a wide variety of influenzas? I may look "clean," but she has no idea what diseases I may carry.

She was obviously starving. Glancing back, I noticed that this skinny young girl is pregnant—maybe seven months. My heart went out to her and her unborn child. I distinctly remember eating like a hay hand when I was carrying my babies. The pregnant girls here receive no extra portions, although they do receive a small, school-size carton of milk with each meal.

I wonder what will become of her baby.

July 31, 2002

Dear DOC Zone Director:

Today two of my daughters came to see me with their baby daughters. It's always a joy to see their beautiful faces, and we had a great visit until the sergeant and the COI, the visiting room officers, sternly ordered me away from the girls and into the visiting room office.

The sergeant began, "We have a no contact rule here." Since I had no idea what he meant and stood there looking stupid, he continued, "You cannot touch your visitors during a visit. But you can hold children under six. Once they've turned six, you can't touch them."

Stunned, I asked, "You mean I can't touch my children?"

He replied, "Oh, you can hold hands, but that's all. You get a brief hug and kiss before a visit and at the end, but there will be no contact during the visit."

I explained that I have been visiting family in prison visiting rooms for almost sixteen and a half years, and no one had ever told me I couldn't touch my children until today. (We have known for several years that we cannot even casually touch our husbands/boyfriends.) He said he understood and that was why he was telling me now. So I had my one warning, and I would be watched.

I left the office only to meet the frightened expressions on my daughters' faces. While explaining the rule and holding back the tears, I watched the hurt and sadness settle on my sweet girls. The rest of the visit was awkward because it's not easy for the three of us to care for a curious thirteen-month-old and a crawling nine-month-old without touching in some manner, however slight.

After they departed and before I could even get back to my housing unit, I heard from other women who've had similar admonitions in the past few weeks. "Do not braid your daughter's hair." "Do not hug him even though he fell down and is crying." "Do not let your daughter sit on your lap. She's seven and too old for that." "Your daughter is eleven and cannot stand there with her arms around your waist." "Do not put your arm around your mother's/grandmother's/aunt's shoulder."

Why have you not heard complaints from these women? Because they are scared, illiterate, or both. I am neither.

Sir, we are all painfully aware that we're in prison and not at home, but why punish our families with such strict rules when we are only trying to maintain family ties and a semblance of normalcy? A staff person told me that one reason for the strict no contact rules is to discourage visits since our visiting room is not

160

adequate for our ever-growing, overcrowded population. It's not our families' fault that the facility is not big enough for the number of women held here.

The last time my grandson came to visit, he sat on my lap while we played Monopoly. Jace was eight then, and we had a great time, and there was nothing wrong with that. There still is nothing wrong with that, but it's prohibited now.

One of my inmate friends has a daughter who will turn seven in a month or so. The inmate has been in prison since her daughter was a baby. The mom always braids her daughter's hair while the little girl sits on her lap. It's a ritual—their time together. It's a joy to behold. Why do you want to take that closeness away from them?

It does my heart good to witness inmates spontaneously hug their mothers and grandmothers. When Carlene's very ill mother visited for the last time right before she died, I can't imagine the guard ordering them not to touch. Carlene and her mother clung to each other the whole visit, knowing it was the last time they'd see each other on this earth.

Those expressions of affection are gifts from God, but now I won't see that anymore? What is happening here? Is this what the Department of Corrections wants? Do you want our visitors to feel unwelcome, nervous, and stiff? Do you want our children to feel unloved?

This camp has become so very cruel, but it pains me more than I can say when the meanness is spread to our innocent loved ones who make the choice to travel here and endure all the hassle required to get in to see us. They do not deserve inhumane treatment.

August 20, 2002

Dearest Momma and Daddy,

Donna left yesterday—to a halfway house—after about a dozen years with us. Bless her heart, her feet never touched the ground as she ran around hugging all her friends goodbye. Everyone had to cry because she was practically bursting with happiness, excitement, and terror—and it's so difficult to bid farewell to a running buddy you'll more than likely never see again.

Don't know if I ever told you, but myopic Donna, her abusive ex, and a friend were inebriated and arguing when Donna accidently ran over and killed her friend. I think she actually was aiming at her ex—but she didn't have her glasses on.

Donna accepted a twenty-year plea bargain, but after she arrived at Renz, she listened to the old cons who told her she had taken too much time for the crime. So she filled out a Form 40 and went back to court. It's not always a good idea to vacate a sentence, because sometimes a person receives a larger sentence the second time. That's exactly what happened to poor Donna. She came back to Renz from her court outcount with thirty years!

When I worked at the law library, I used Donna as my prime example when any girl with less than a life sentence asked about appeals. "Don't know what you've got until it's gone."

As soon as I met Donna, I recognized her intelligence and potential and enrolled her in Lincoln University classes. She was not raised in a ghetto environment. She came from good people and kept a good job. Later when the computer programming class opened up, she started it with me. We shared a cell and worked in the same shop for years.

Donna used to crack me up. She'd shake her head when one of her Black sisters talked or acted stereotypically "Black." Sometimes in a class or a meeting, she'd look around and observe, "Why am I the only Black person in this room?"

Donna is so ornery. Remember the scarecrow's song from *The Wizard of Oz,* "If I Only Had a Brain?" Donna whistled it softly as background music when anyone acted stupidly. It was our inside joke.

When Larry, our beloved computer programming instructor, suffered heart failure in the middle of a coding class and actually died in the ISU trailer at Church Farm Renz, Donna and I became the Two Stooges in our inept attempt to simultaneously squeeze through the exit door. Our supervisor Kathy calmly told us that

Larry was experiencing a health problem and that we needed to return to our dorm immediately so the ambulance could come in the gate and we panicked. There was this awful gravity to her order that scared us, so we tripped over each other in an attempt to leave the building. As we scurried past his desk, his ashen ill face froze our hearts. That's a day neither of us will forget.

Momma, I know you remember when Donna's mother passed away. Jessie was such a character. Donna may never truly get over that loss. She loved her mother with a passion—her father, too. Since Donna was not permitted to attend either funeral by DOC policy, Father Behan dedicated a special memorial service for each of them. Donna used to call Father B a "Baptist priest" because he can surely preach the gospel!

When Donna first told me she had been diagnosed as manic depressive, I observed, "Oh, shoot, Donna, all people have their highs and lows. Life is one big roller coaster ride. Experiences are fantastically wonderful or unbelievably horrible—and everything in between. In my opinion, every human is bipolar. My solution is to take your vitamins, exercise, and keep busy." She could only shake her head.

After Gary and I fell in love, I had a big crying fit all over Donna. Gary's such a wonderful man and it hurts so much to realize that he's now committed to a woman who's in prison forever. Although Donna simply detests emotional breakdowns, she listened to me rant and rave and patiently talked some sense into me. We've been through flood, famine, pestilence, and more together.

August 30, 2002

Dear Marsha,

On Thursday, August 22, I was granted my first opportunity to visit my friend Faye Copeland, who was sequestered in the infirmary. Faye is eighty-one, was on death row, and several years ago through the appeals process had her sentence changed to life with no parole.

I never saw that as much of a victory myself, especially for a good woman who was a victim of her husband's abuse. Ray Copeland murdered itinerant farmhands near Chillicothe, and both he and Faye received the death penalty in the late '80s.

Faye recently has had two strokes and is paralyzed on her left side. It hurt me to know that she was all alone in her cell most of the time.

Last week I asked my caseworker to see if I could visit her. I also asked Sister Fran, our chaplain volunteer. Sister Fran suggested that I call Faye's attorney to urge him to work on a medical parole for her, but Kent informed me that due to her no parole status, the only relief she is legally afforded would be from the governor.

Last Thursday morning my boss received a call for me to go to the Infirmary. When I arrived, the officer frisked me as he warned, "You have thirty minutes—not one second more." He then walked me down the corridor, unlocked the big steel door to Faye's stark stall, and let me in.

As I eased around the hospital bed, I noticed that her fragile skin was bruised black from the IVs. One side of her face sagged as if it were not related to my Faye. Tears welled up, but I fought them back so Faye wouldn't see my grief.

Years ago, I teasingly called myself Queen Sassafras, and Faye quipped, "Queen Sassy Ass, I'd say."

When I leaned down with my face close to hers, I greeted her with, "Hi, Faye. It's Queen Sassy Ass."

I feared she wouldn't recognize me, but she instantly grabbed my hand and whispered, "I love you, Patty. I was praying for you to come see me."

We chatted while I stroked her hair, face, and arm. Everyone longs for physical contact. Loving touch is much needed—especially for a person who is in pain and locked up alone in a cell.

I asked if she wanted to share a prayer, and before I could get started, she took off praying for her family. Her biggest concern is that her children and their families can overcome the stigma of being direct descendants of Faye and Ray Copeland. Sometimes I could understand her words, and sometimes I could not—but I know God understood, and that's all that matters.

Poor Faye prayed for over fifteen minutes. The IV in her leg was so painful that she kept reaching for it with her one good hand as if to shoo the pain away. She prayed so hard that she fell asleep almost immediately after I whispered, "In Jesus' name we pray, Amen."

I kept an eye on my wristwatch, because I wanted to end our visit gently and naturally when it was time—not abruptly when the guard hollered.

Looking around the cell, I noticed the one small, barred window high up on the outside wall—too high for anyone to look out and see the trees across the road or even the sky that belongs to us all. The room was plain white-painted concrete blocks. There was not one article in the room that belonged to Faye.

A stainless-steel combination lavatory and commode stood ready in one corner. Fluorescent lights hung glaring over us from the high white ceiling. Prison sounds were all I heard: steel doors slamming, keys jingling, endless transmissions from the guard's walkie-talkie, heavy booted footsteps, indistinct conversation.

My heart ached to decorate her space with flowers, balloons, cards, and the things my own mother had in her hospital room when she was ill—so that when Faye awoke, she'd be able to look around and see evidence that she is loved and not forgotten in spite of her dire circumstance. I also wanted to bring in a radio—something to add music and block out the prison clatter and echoes.

Stroking her gently as she slept, I softly slipped out with three minutes to spare.

Numbly I made my way back to work. An extraordinarily marked and vibrantly colored butterfly appeared before me and danced in my path just long enough to ease my mind and soothe my heart. Just like the unknowing caterpillar in the cocoon, we have no idea what wonders await us when this life is done.

When I made it back to work, my boss informed me that while I was gone my caseworker had called and reported that I could not visit Faye under any circumstances. He became a bit flustered to hear that I was with her at that very moment.

This week I was granted permission for daily thirty-minute visits with Faye. Some days she slept through our whole visit, so I would gently pray over her and softly sing old hymns. On some level she knew I was there.

Today news that Faye had miraculously been granted medical parole blazed across the prison camp. Most everyone was overjoyed, and many wept to know that our dear friend would not die alone in a cold cell in prison.

I was blessed with the opportunity to say goodbye. Approaching her bed for the final time, I asked, "Faye, did they tell you that you're going home today?"

She answered weakly, "Not all the way," referring to the fact that she was going to a nursing home. We held hands while I pointed out, "Faye, before this day is done, you'll be breathing FREE air! That's a miracle!"

And it is a miracle. A wonderful prison miracle. Faye will not die in a cold prison cell. Sister Fran, a host of attorneys, the chairman of the Missouri Board of Probation and Parole, the staff at the retirement village in Chillicothe, and many others worked on this miracle of compassion.

By my calculations, Faye's ambulance should have made it to the nursing home by now. I bet she's tucked into a crisp, clean bed in the middle of an inviting room surrounded by smiling loved ones. Hope someone brought balloons!

December 1, 2002

Dear Carrie,

Unfortunately, our prison population currently suffers from an epidemic of STAPH INFECTION. We've been warned to be careful, wash our hands, etc. The cleaners have washed everything down with a weak chlorine bleach solution—too weak to be of actual benefit, but strong enough to smell as if it were.

It's my understanding that most prisons in many states are also experiencing the same plague—one of the many hazards of communal living in overcrowded, unclean conditions.

Yesterday a young girl slid in next to me on the bench at canteen and asked, "Miss Patty, have you heard about this terrible disease, this infection all the staff have?" (When I grew to be middle-aged, the young girls here began calling me Miss Patty. It's a sign of respect used for the elderly. I hate it.)

While trying not to laugh out loud because she was totally sincere, I advised, "That's why I stay at least an arm's length away from them. A STAFF INFECTION is no joke."

"Yeah, that's a good idea, Miss Patty. You be so smart."

Smart aleck is more like it!

Thursday, January 30, 2003

Dear Gary,

What a prison day! First of all the canteen computer was down, so no one could shop. (Those with nicotine, caffeine, and sugar habits are jonesing.) Then there was a fire drill on 2 House a little after 1 pm, and they couldn't count right—so at a little after 2 pm everyone on camp was ordered back into their cells for a big recount. By the time that impromptu count cleared, it was too late to go back to work. Then after supper the worst thing happened: THE GOON SQUAD STRUCK!

They drove their vans around back behind our housing unit and stealthily converged on C wing as I watched from my window. Lord, how I hate the attack of the goon squad. They always terrorize a dorm. I'm not kidding.

Dressed in black to intimidate and mimic ninjas or Special Forces guys, they have different methods of starting the night of torture, but the end result is always the same. Everything we own, our meager possessions, are tossed in the air, discarded, or lost in the shuffle. These officers would make great sackers and looters since they obviously enjoy the search and destroy aspect of this job.

They also yell and scream and bark orders at everyone like crazed drill sergeants, their faces distorted. The new gals trembled in fear of the unknown. We old gals trembled for the fear of the known. When we saw them hit C wing, our hearts went out to our friends over there, and at the same time, we breathed a tentative sigh of relief to be spared for the time being. The prospect that we could be the next victims loomed over us like a black cloud of tear gas.

While the goons tore up C wing, we were on lockdown status and couldn't leave our cells. Shellie sprawled on the floor inside our door and watched the action down the hall in the rotunda using my mirror—an old jail trick. She offered a running commentary of status reports. Rox sat perched on her bunk like nothing was happening, answering letters and blocking out the turmoil. Sandy feverishly crocheted a baby afghan as if her life depended on it. Mickie sauntered over to my bunk and watched my TV. (Yes, you counted right. We now have five people in the four-person rooms because of the overcrowding.) I paced the length of the room and peered through the bars of the cell window in order to catch any action on the other wing. Nerve-racking, that's what it is, just plain nerve-racking.

My captive friends and I swapped old stories of previous raids—except Rox, who ignored it all. A few years ago, I was on a visit with you when the goons hit my wing. After you had to leave me, and I was strip searched, I trudged back to the housing unit then casually quipped to a guard, "Quite a night."

She quickly grabbed me by the shoulder, spun me around, slammed my face into the concrete block wall, and roughly frisked me. Admittedly I felt stunned, shocked, and shaken. I didn't move fast enough for her, so she screamed in my face, "GET TO YOUR ROOM NOW!" Two male officers joined in, and the chorus hurled this directive at me as I hurried stumbling down the cluttered hall to the door of my cell.

The entire hall was piled with the litter of cardboard boxes, toilet paper, state blankets, magazines, sanitary napkins, catalogs, popcorn, potato chips, plastic containers. My roomies and neighbors were all silently lined up in the hall with their foreheads pressed against either wall. These ladies had been there in that position for hours with no break. No one was allowed to use the bathroom for any reason.

I found a spot near Donna, and as I leaned forward to also place my forehead on the concrete block, she frantically mouthed to me that she might pee her pants. Several of the ladies were old and not well. They looked shaky, as if they might crumple onto the floor any minute. The compassionate, kind-hearted part of me felt like crying. The warrior part of me felt like fighting. I gave in to neither.

They began that madness a little after 6 pm, but it was after midnight before we were permitted to go back to our trashed cells to begin the cleanup process. Too weary to complain, the only sound was the rustling of sorting clothes, bedding, papers, and plastics. Some of the ladies were in the toilet, shamefully attempting to clean themselves. They were the poor souls who had been unable to wait all those hours to use the bathroom. No showers were allowed. According to housing unit rules, the showers are off limits after 10 pm.

My roomies and I numbly searched for our things in the rubble. We made our beds with sticky sheets stained with substances such as spilled instant coffee, baby oil, and loose laundry detergent. We went through papers trying to salvage letters and drawings from our children—and legal documents.

The not-so-lucky ones were called to the dayroom to receive conduct violations for too many craft items, etc. I received one for "dangerous contraband": a plastic drafting triangle. I'd used it while housed at Church Farm Renz. The Maintenance Department had commissioned me to crank out technical architectural plans of the prison. In fact, I was paid $25 for three months' eye-straining, tedious labor.

Since Maintenance still called upon me on occasion to draw up plans, I kept the drafting tool in my possession. To wiggle out of that write-up, I did some tall talking. Believe me! But no one wanted to believe me. They firmly suspected that I was lying and intended to use that hunk of plastic to either escape or as a lethal weapon. They longed to stuff me in the hole as punishment.

At Chillicothe in the mid '80s, I heard that a goon squad guy actually caused a girl's arm to fracture when he shoved her, and she toppled down the stairs. Rumor had it that she nervously giggled when she saw them. That's how crazed they get. We are never to smile or laugh at them, no matter how silly they appear or how nervous we become. In fact, we never call them the goon squad to their faces. They take themselves VERY seriously.

Also, they do not have to follow any personal property policies. They simply throw away anything they want. It matters not if the item is allowed by prison rules. If a goon wants to toss it, it's gone. No argument. No paperwork. No recourse. No shit.

In 1988 I was standing at the top of the stairs rummaging in the utility closet for a broom when they surprised us. A big boy leaped almost on top of me, shouting. Startled, I thought he was asking for a broom, "GET ME A BROOM!" I tried to obey and hand him one, which angered him even more, "YOU HEARD ME. GET ME A BROOM!"

That goon was so mad and so close that my face was covered with spittle. Then it dawned on my terrified soul that he was saying, "GET TO YOUR ROOM!" My heart raced even faster than my skinny legs to follow his order, while the other squad members assaulted our floor, taking no hostages. That was another sorry prison night.

In the '80s the squad marched like Nazis, but dressed like big, militant pumpkins in orange jumpsuits with black riot helmets, brandishing nightsticks. In the summer of '86, the first night I heard them stomp down the sidewalk, I peered out the window, and my hair stood straight up.

Having no idea who they were, I instinctively knew this wasn't good. As soon as the marching stopped at the end of my hall, the head goon announced, "THROW ALL YOUR CONTRABAND OUT YOUR DOOR! NOW!" Hearing thuds and crashes, my cellie and I looked around for something to contribute, but we two newbies weren't sure what contraband actually was, so we huddled silently.

After motionless hours of listening to the mayhem, the stomping recommenced. Oh, hallelujah! They were leaving. We cracked our door open to peek into the hall, saw it was relatively safe, and thanked God we had been spared. As we made a much-needed trip to the bathroom, I thought that this must be a tiny sample of the fear the innocent Jews felt during Hitler's reign of terror. You're thinking, "She's overly dramatic." But until you live through one of these raids, don't pass judgment.

Never in all my locked-up years have I seen or even heard that the goons found anything of worth at the camp where I reside. No weapons. No drugs. Hardly seems worth the effort and expense, but I suppose finding contraband is not actually the goal. If their objective is to make certain we never ever forget where we are and who we are, they are right on target. Mission accomplished.

February 1, 2003

Dear Nancy,

I'm worried about my friend J. R. You may remember him from when I was a programming student. When all our teachers either quit or died, J. R. was given the assignment to complete our instruction in the art of computer programming over a closed-circuit TV. Why via television? Because J. R. is an inmate at the Walls, the dilapidated original men's prison in Jefferson City—a bank robber, I believe.

When we had no one, J. R. stepped up to the plate—and did not strike out. Can you imagine attempting to teach a dozen diverse women an extremely difficult and technical skill from a distance? J. R. is a born teacher, and maybe the smartest person I ever met.

Oh, and on top of all that, J. R. is legally blind! Now that I think about what transpired, it is another prison miracle that we graduated and became the excellent "code busters" we are today.

Once during class, Mickie started crying from the frustration invoked by the complexity of that particular lesson. J. R. peered into the TV, trying to figure out what was happening on our side. When we told him that he'd made Mickie cry, he went right on with the lesson as if everything was fine. You know men aren't good with tears. To paraphrase Tom Hanks in that baseball movie, "There are no tears in programming."

In defiance, the whole class turned around with our backs to the camera and our arms crossed. It was our way of teaching our teacher. Our group would not continue if Mickie was disabled. Lame ducks are not abandoned by the flock.

J. R. is no dummy, and quickly learned his lesson. He called a smoke break. When we returned, our properly chastised master patiently explained the elusive point to Mickie and the rest of us.

We all grew to love J. R. as our mentor and big brother. He never let us down and worked tirelessly to hammer home concepts and logic—and always treated us respectfully. J. R. is a good man, a good friend. In fact, he's my age, only two days older. He and Gary have become good phone friends, too. They are both originally southern boys, J.R. from South Carolina. Gary commented that J.R. has a great laugh—booming and infectious. I agree. As J. R. would say, "Indeed."

Recently J. R. was diagnosed with cancer of the esophagus and began chemo and radiation. His parole date is in 2004, and his application for medical parole was denied, so he's undergoing all these painful procedures as a cuffed and shackled inmate.

J. R. is a mountain of a man—really tall and big, but recently he's lost a huge amount of weight with this illness and treatment. J. R. is also a mountain man in his heart and yearns to return to the Rockies of Colorado from whence he came over twenty years ago.

My hope for J. R. is that he beats the odds and makes it home to his snow-covered Rocky Mountains so he can breathe fresh, free, thin Colorado air once again.

Wednesday, February 5, 2003

Dearest Gary,

Everyone is suffering from sleep deprivation today. That's because we were rousted out of our bunks near midnight for another dreaded fire drill.

Many are under the assumption that a fire drill has something to do with fire—the possibility of fire anyway. Oh no. Not a prison fire drill. Let me explain.

If the powers-that-be were concerned that we might perish from smoke or blaze, we would be schooled in the art of fire prevention and how to make our way to safety. In all the years I've been locked up, I've heard of no such training, much less received any. "Stop, drop, and roll" is not taught in prison. But for real, what would burn in a metal/cement environment?

A fire drill is another weapon in their arsenal. It's another tool in their box of "Ways to Make Sure They Know Who's Boss."

When a fire drill is called, we are all to rush outside as fast as we can. Then we stand in line. The officers yell at us, and count us, and yell at us, and count us until they've had their fill—sometimes for hours in all kinds of unpleasant weather. Only then can we return grumbling to our interrupted day.

A few months ago, the fire drill was called during the evening. Shelley was in the shower—the worst place to be at that particular time. (I never ever take a shower without the fear that a fire drill will be called before I can finish.) She was screamed at and forced to rush outside and stand in line for nearly an hour dripping wet, with only a bathrobe and plastic shower shoes to protect her from the elements. I was freezing, and I was fully dressed. None of the officers showed one bit of compassion for her and the others like her shivering. Shelley was hardly the only poor woman caught in the shower.

In the winter of '86, I shared a room with an elderly lady who shot and killed her longtime cheating husband as he walked to his vehicle after leaving his paramour's bed. Then she suffered a severe stroke. (If memory serves me right, Edith served about six years on her ten-year sentence for the premeditated murder.)

As punishment for general and widespread unruly behavior in our dorm that winter, we were subjected to fire drills in the dead of nearly every night. To exit the dorm, we had to descend a rickety, ice-covered metal fire escape. Poor Edith—the stairs scared her to death, because she had so little control of one leg and arm.

One cold night when the alarm sounded, I suggested to Edith that we hide out in the closet and not participate in the fire drill. (In those days we weren't counted until we were back in our cells.)

Reluctantly she agreed. Although Edith had mustered up the gumption to "take care of" her unfaithful mate, she was hardly a rebel. But fear of slipping down that fire escape supplied her heart with the courage to follow my defiant plan.

We silently and safely hid in the warm closet while our comrades froze in the snow drifts. As soon as I heard clomping, we reappeared and acted as if we, too, were just coming in—an Academy Award worthy performance, I might add.

While housed at Church Farm Renz, a scorned lover lit fire to a bathrobe belonging to the object of her desire. The robe never actually blazed. It smoldered, and when we realized what was causing the awful smell—while the officer feverishly thumbed through his code book to find the number of that particular emergency so he could call it in on the radio—an inmate simply pulled it off the bedpost and stomped the fire out. That's as close to an actual fire that I've ever seen in prison.

One summer I witnessed a woman faint from heat exhaustion during a fire drill. We were forced to stand in the blazing sun, but Vera had recently undergone major surgery and told the officer that she felt like she wouldn't be able to stay on her feet. Her predicament fell on deaf ears. About an hour into the drill she collapsed, and the officers were totally surprised.

If you think that at this camp we use fire exits for fire drills, you're wrong. We did that once about five years ago when we first arrived, but the fire exit doors have no ramps, and the ladies confined to wheelchairs had no way to roll to the ground. The pusher of the wheelchair in front of me gave up and just spilled her handicapped rider out the door. It wasn't pretty. Since that one fiasco, all four wings of our housing unit crowd thread through one door to the outside.

Saturday, February 8, 2003

Dear Mary,

Tonight, while waiting to go to supper, I witnessed a whole new level of prison insanity. You'll be hard-pressed to believe this one.

After 4:30 pm count clears, those of us who are hungry, that includes me, lurk in the dayroom so we can be one of the first from our wing to get out the door to walk halfway across the camp to the chow hall. It's the root, hog, or die philosophy. Also, most halt right outside the door to flick their Bics. They can't seem to walk and light a cigarette at the same time. It's best to get ahead of the smokers' traffic jam.

Tonight, the very young sergeant burst in importantly and made this announcement: "FROM NOW ON NO OFFENDER CAN BRING TOILET PAPER TO THE CHOW HALL. YOU WILL RECEIVE A CDV FOR DISOBEYING A DIRECT ORDER IF YOU TRY TO. THIS CAME FROM THE LIEU-TENANT!" The girls on A wing nicknamed this sargeant Chia Pet because of his hair, but the girls on C wing call him Woody, the cowboy from *Toy Story,* because of his build. Prisoners, just like schoolchildren, tend to come up with nicknames for certain officers. I've noticed that if an officer has the good sense to act like a human being, usually no nickname is used—or if one is, it's a nice one. But the officers who warrant disrespect are awarded nicknames or are just plain called names.

This is the same guard who recently gave us a big lecture about "no sagging." "WE WILL NOT ALLOW SAGGING ON THIS CAMP." In case you're as clueless as I was, sagging is the way young people wear their trousers way down on their hips, so it appears as though they are hauling around a fully loaded diaper. As he droned on about the evils of sagging, I looked down at my chest acting flustered, "How can he write me up for sagging? Hasn't he ever heard of gravity and the aging process? Sagging is not my fault!"

Anyway, the dayroom mob grumbled, because we've always rolled off a bit of stiff, state toilet paper to use as napkins. This is done purely in self-defense. When a loaded tray is shoved out of the chow window counter, the tray becomes a mess of food slime as it slides toward you. Therefore, when one of us picks up the tray, a messy hand is certain.

It's bad enough that we are forced to eat almost like animals. The only utensil provided is a spork—a tablespoon-sized orange plastic spoon with cut-out zigzags on the tip. If meat is served, we must pick it up with our hands and tear it. Forget any table manners, if you were ever taught. And eating soup with this spork becomes a comedy routine. The liquid falls through the cut-out tip before it can reach your hungry mouth! We must lean down close to the soup and try to catch it before it falls back in the tray. But that's really a whole different story. Back to prison napkins, aka toilet paper.

After Woody bellowed our new rule, he ordered us to line up for pat searches. He inspected us to make sure none of the forbidden toilet paper would leave his housing unit. He takes this job extremely seriously—making the world safe from paper-packing prisoners.

A watery-eyed, scarlet-nosed, elderly lady asked nasally, "What if you have a 'code' and need to blow your 'node'?"

"I don't care. No toilet paper in the chow hall for any reason."

So, Woody made a show of searching the girls who offered themselves to him. The rest of us hung back. I brought my stash of illegal toilet paper with me, in violation of the brand-new rule, although I didn't flaunt it. Discreetly, after the meal, I wiped my hands with the contraband and shoved it in my coat pocket.

Now we have to sneak to keep clean and neat. Where do they get these ideas?

February 23, 2003

Dear Dale,

At this particular prison, those of us who have been violation-free for at least ninety days are eligible for food visits, visits where the visitor is permitted to bring in a meal. Food visits are set up every quarter—two days per housing unit—although I've heard they soon will cut us down to twice a year. This week was my turn.

Now food visits are not all rosy. Our families have a whole list of rules and regulations regarding the kind of food, the kind and size of containers the food can come in, and the number of items. Most of the rules make no sense at all—like when the guards count those little individual condiment packages, like catsup or hot sauce, as a food item.

Our family cannot bring us any meat with bones. We've been told that we might smuggle a chicken leg back to our room and fashion a weapon from it. But we are served chicken with bones in the prison chow hall—and the visiting room vending machines sell chicken wings that have bones. So, all bones are safe except the ones your momma might bring in.

The fruit rule makes no sense either. We cannot have fresh fruit on a visit. The theory is that liquor could be injected into the fruit—I guess like vodka in a watermelon, but who would pack the whole melon?

I remember at Church Farm Renz when a guard would not allow any fruit pies for the big Thanksgiving food visit. Luckily the superintendent showed up, and Janie told him that all these old ladies had made pies—and the front desk guard had kept them. When Janie and the superintendent confronted the guard, he lamely stuttered, "Buh, buh, but they are fresh baked fruit pies, and they cuh, cuh, can't have fresh fruit." In no time at all, the superintendent and Janie stood at the door handing out pies to the grateful bakers in the room. Sheesh!

On the last food visit, Gary brought his world-famous chili, but the plastic bowl he carried it in was an inch too deep according to the policy, so he was forced to ladle chili into the disposable plastic bowls he'd brought and carry all the bowls in separately. This is why I try to discourage him from going through all this insanity.

Attempting to convince Gary to NOT take a day off work to feed me on this food visit proved futile, as always. He said he'd be here Thursday at 10 am—and at 10:20 am, my name was called for a visit. I anxiously flew over to the strip search area.

Once inside the visiting room, I scanned the bustling room and found my tall, handsome man grinning from ear to ear. I turned from the check-in officer to walk into Gary's arms when I caught a glimpse of Daddy standing behind the post. I jumped straight up with surprise and joy then jumped into Daddy's arms instead. I had NO idea Gary was bringing my folks!

The realization that my parents are growing old does not sit easily with me. Daddy shouldn't drive this far after dark, so I don't get the opportunity to see them as often as we'd like. Gary's so thoughtful to bring them with him.

Taking Daddy's sweet face in my hands, I kissed him. He looked sharp in a brightly colored and striped cowboy shirt and new blue Wranglers held up with a tooled-leather belt and ornate big silver buckle. It still seems odd to see Daddy without his Stetson, but hats are not allowed for anyone in the visiting room—visitors included.

Then I turned to hug my beautiful mother—Momma's hugs are as cushy as Daddy's are hard. Momma was wearing a feminine, wine-colored blouse and matching earrings. As always, her lipstick and nail polish also matched.

When it was Gary's turn, I squeezed him tight and grilled him, "How long have you known you were bringing Momma and Daddy? Did you know when I spoke to you on the phone Monday? Did Sarah know?"

Gary chuckled as he bent down to give me our one allowed greeting kiss and smugly bragged, "Yes, it was a big family secret, and amazingly nobody told." That was amazing in my family, where everyone tells everything.

Momma had fixed a delicious pork roast with potatoes, onions, and carrots. I hadn't had Momma's cooking in years. Gary contributed his famous broccoli casserole and boiled a big bowl of shrimp, too. Daddy and I shared a pint of Ben and Jerry's finest right off the bat, before it could melt. They stuffed me.

At count time we inmates were ordered to line up. I stood not far from my table, so I introduced my young red-headed friend Toni, "Momma, Daddy, this is Toni. She works with me."

Momma shook her head, "No, don't want to get too close to anyone else. I'll end up writing her, and I write too many as it is— Rox, Mickie,...." We were howling. Momma is SO funny! Later she asked about Toni. Momma's a sucker for girls in trouble.

As three guards walked up and down counting and recounting the line of inmates, I caught Daddy's expression and read his sharp cowboy mind, "They are sure making a big dad-burned chore out of a little job."

When I returned to the table, Daddy offered his opinion, "Those guards sure would be up a creek during roundup if they can't count a few stationary lined-up women. What would they do if they had to count a herd that's running from one corral to another—and get an accurate number by steers and heifers—on the first and only try? They'd never pull that off." I thought to myself that they wouldn't be able to manage a roundup anyway. Too much hard work.

About once an hour we are allowed outside in the small, fenced visiting yard for a short "smoke break." Daddy wanted to stretch his legs, so we all went out for some fresh air. When my folks inadvertently stepped too close to the fence, one guard was quick to holler. We must stay at least three feet away from the inner fence.

That peeved look took over Momma's lovely face as she asked, "Do they really think your dad and I are going to hop up there and climb both those fences to get to our car? Don't they know we're leaving the same way we came in?" Momma lives in a land of common sense where seventy-four-year-old ladies don't climb razor-wire fences for any reason—a land far, far from prison.

My tender-hearted neighbor Pam, an RN and recovering heroin addict, later told me that when I helped Momma with her sweater and fixed her up to leave, she almost cried because me fussing over Momma was so sweet and loving. It was a perfect prison day.

Thursday, March 27, 2003

Dear Nancy,

We were all excited because former State Representative Dale Whiteside was granted a March 26 meeting with the governor's chief counsel to discuss the clemency applications for the five of us he's sponsoring—and has been working diligently to help for over a decade. Dale planned to bring along Helen, my old friend who was granted executive clemency by Governor John Ashcroft and paroled in '94. They have been working for two years to secure a meeting with this current administration.

Helen told me to call her last night after the meeting to get the scoop, but when I called, the first words she spoke were, "Patty, I'm so sorry." It turned out that the meeting was cancelled. The governor's secretary left that message on Dale's voicemail the night before, but Dale's dear wife missed that particular transmission.

So, Dale, Marilou, Helen, Helen's daughter, granddaughter, and son-in-law converged on Jefferson City unknowingly. Dale and his wife lived in the northwest part of the state outside Chillicothe. Helen and her family live in St. Louis.

Helen had a Yugoslavian "conniption fit" about the cancellation. She planned to present notarized copies of affidavits from Judge Beaird (yes, Bob's a judge now) and Cardarella stating that our defense team was indeed offered a plea agreement—one by which I would have served six or seven years in prison, not fifty. The affidavits also stated that the trial would have certainly turned out differently if the defense team had known about the stranger who stalked our home the night of the murder.

Recently Sarah said that someone who stumbled upon the website she designed for us emailed a message comparing my case to that of the man whom the police thought had nabbed Elizabeth Smart—the guy who died in jail. It turned out that he had nothing to do with the Utah kidnapping, but the police stopped looking when they found him. If the Johnson County police had paid attention to the lead concerning the man in the white sedan who lurked near our home the night of Bill's murder, they might have found Bill's killer. But they stopped investigating only a few hours after they decided I was the easiest suspect.

Yesterday my friends took off from work and drove many miles for nothing. The team all felt hurt, disappointed, and frustrated. (By the way, speaking of jobs, did I ever tell you that Helen is the office manager of a huge law firm in the city? That's a major accomplishment for anyone, much less an ex-con!) Helen also took her frustration a step further to just plain anger at the way peon taxpayers are treated by politicians.

Helen's son-in-law has never toured the capitol, so they showed him around since they were there and had no meeting to attend. Someone in their party suggested that they drive by our ruined, flooded-out prison, Renz Farm. When Becky caught sight of what's left of the camp, the color drained from her sweet, pretty face. She experienced such a strong emotional response that she became sick to her stomach.

Later Becky confessed to her mother, "You don't know how awful it was to visit you there, Mom, and have to leave you in that place. Can you imagine leaving your mother in a prison camp? After each visit, I sobbed my heart out all the way home—without you to hold and soothe me and wipe away my tears. For thirteen long years, I lived in sorrow and pain without you."

While Helen told me what Becky told her, tears welled up in my own eyes. My incarceration is also a punishment to my children, my whole family. My children have been forced to say goodbye to me and leave me behind bars and inside the razor-wire fence at the end of every visit for seventeen years, since they were little kids.

Now my four grown children all have children of their own to visit their granny in prison. These sweet, innocent victims have started a whole new generation to mourn and cry over me.

Every visit is wonderful in that we can see each other and share, but also every visit is absolute torture because they must leave without their mother. The kisses and hugs at the conclusion of a visit invariably become desperate and anguished—and embarrassing because guards are staring. Every time I see my family, we part with tears of heartache.

July 6, 2003

Dear Mary,

Tuesday afternoon a special inmate council meeting was called to discuss the sharp rise in the number of violent exchanges. The fact that we're overcrowded, short staffed, have fewer recreational periods in which to blow off steam—all contributing factors to the creation of this pressure-cooker effect—were somehow overlooked.

All our problems are our very own fault, according to the administration and custody. The associate superintendent even had the nerve to tell the council representatives that all the staff work here simply and expressly to help us—not for the paycheck, "We sure don't work here for the money." I always felt in my heart that the staff would work here for free—that's how much they love us.

Recently one disgruntled cellmate smashed in the head of her sleeping bunkmate with the sleeper's own TV and nearly killed her. Several fights have broken out with everyone armed with a lock-in-a-sock as the weapon of choice. A heavy combination lock in the toe of a long, state-issued tube sock is quite effective when swung expertly at an enemy's skull.

The prison officials' solution was to call in the regional goon squads for a huge raid. Starting at 8 am on Wednesday, all the inmates were herded to the gym. Soon officers noticed there was not enough room in the little half-gym, so grumbling women were herded out to the recreation yard. Nearly 1,700 women waited hours and hours while goons tore up the housing units. The line to the four-stall toilet was ten times worse than the line to the ladies' room at a Cardinals game.

Gary showed up in the middle of the mayhem for my birthday visit, so I escaped most of the madness. He carried on his birthday tattoo tradition with the number 54 encircled in a heart drawn on his arm with red marker. After Gary left, I spent the remainder of the day cleaning up and reorganizing my small "tossed" living area. But it could have been worse. I've seen worse.

Oh, by the way, no weapons of mass destruction were found.

On Independence Day, all the inmates in the 9 am med line, who get a dose of Prozac, were inadvertently given another medication, a strong sedative. By eleven, women were falling out all over camp. It was an epidemic. Mickie and loads of others couldn't walk and were all wheeled to medical. There are only so many wheelchairs on camp, so the rest slowly dragged themselves across camp looking like zombies blindly and haltingly trudging from the graveyard. It was the Day of the Living Dead. The 11:30 count was not commenced until after noon because the zombies were so doggone slow. I'm talking around 100 dead women walking.

Fourteen were taken to the nearest hospital, thirty miles away. Mick's blood pressure bottomed out, so she alone was quickly ambulanced. Because of her severe Hep C, her liver didn't have the power to come to her rescue. Just got her back to her cell this afternoon. We nearly lost her.

September 4, 2003

Dearest Gary,

As I approached the gym door on my way to step aerobics class, the following prison scene unfolded before me.

A short, small, smiling Black woman approached a gossiping group of gray-clad gals who were loitering, smoking—killing time.

"Hey," the happy gal yelled, "I go home ta-marruh! An dey be habin' pancakes fuh breh-fuss. Dey's muh fay-rut! E'ry-tine I go home, dey be habin' pancakes!"

Laughing out loud as I yanked open the heavy steel door, I repeated, "Every time I go home. Ev-er-y doggone time."

November 27, 2003

Dear Mary,

Did I tell you that I've joined a theater class? Toni and Janiece, delightful young girls who work in my shop, urged me into it. The announcement flyer on the bulletin board did not fully describe the class, and from past experience I feared it was just some sort of talent show, so I refrained from signing up. But the girls excitedly explained that the "real" teacher plans on directing a "real" play, so I wormed my way into the class.

And I'm sure glad I did! Agnes, our teacher and guide through the world of acting, is a joy, full of energy, intelligence, love of life, excitement, knowledge, and wonderment! In years she's not a kid, but I really don't know if she's as old as me or not. Agnes's pretty face is ageless, with bright expressive eyes that dance like those of a precocious and yet mischievous child.

Speaking of her eyes, she wears the most distinctive pair of black-framed glasses. When I first spotted them, I mistook them for Harry Potter's, but they aren't round. They are slightly oval vertically, not horizontally, like most spectacles.

Her steel gray hair is cropped short to match her spunky attitude. Petite, the size of a child. A tiny bundle of energy and ideas. Never still for long. When she talks, she uses her whole body—her hands, her feet, every part of her. You'd adore her, too. We all do.

Gary told me that public radio aired a huge story of how she molded a group of rough male prisoners into Shakespearean actors—changing their lives in the process. Well, she plans to whip the same whammy on us. In fact, we've chosen *Macbeth* as our first production, which is aiming pretty high as far as I'm concerned.

It is so much fun, such a departure from our usual prison days. Agnes storms in on Thursday afternoons at 2 pm and transports us to her world until 9 pm when we are forced to part for count. She has total confidence that we will do Shakespeare justice and therefore, so do I.

The class reminded me how much I miss college classes. In '94 Pell grants were outlawed for prisoners, so our higher education folded. A few years ago, a federally funded program was implemented that offers college to those under twenty-five—an attempt to save the young before they morph into hardened criminals. But until now there has been nothing academic for those of us over age. But now I'm back to my true vocation—that of a professional student.

And memorizing all those lines while attempting to not trip over the "hasts" and "thithers" is a challenge. We never use the king's English around here!

One Door Closes and Another Opens

Tuesday, January 27, 2004

Dear Nancy,

Guess what? I'm still in shock! I can hardly believe it!

This morning I lounged in a barber chair in the cosmo classroom while a young student dried my hair and entertained with tales of her plans and aspirations. The vo-tech officer interrupted, "Patty, call your attorney—right now."

I blinked twice before answering, "You must have the wrong person." She disagreed, so I asked, "Call who? I don't actually have an attorney and a number." With that she disappeared, and Shannon returned to my wet hair and her story.

In a moment, the officer shoved a phone to my ear. A female voice explained that my caseworker should have told me about this call last week. She mumbled something about a fax and the superintendent, and I got the impression that this was important. She gave me a phone number to use immediately—with Phil Gibson as the contact name.

We are planning a big surprise birthday party Saturday for Daddy's eightieth (which is really today), and Daddy's former employer and old friend is named Bill Gibson. Surely Bill wasn't calling me in regard to the party. That was my first thought.

The student refused to allow me to go outside in the cold with wet hair, so she feverishly aimed the blow dryer at my head while my feeble brain attempted to figure out what the call was about. The number seemed vaguely familiar, too, which only added to the mystery.

A pleasant woman's voice answered the ring and connected me to Phil Gibson, who wasted no time in telling me the most amazing news. Out of over 800 applications, the Midwest Innocence Project is looking at MY case. YES! Can you believe it?

Mr. Gibson's voice was so kind and gentle as he told me that they've been aware of me for a number of years. Tears welled up in my eyes.

After he stated that he was privy to the late Governor Carnahan's plan to commute my sentence, he went on to say that he also knew that in October the current governor had denied my application for executive clemency, even though I have the best clemency file ever. He referred to that as "the bad decision." But evidently that unjust rejection prompted them to take a hard look at me. One door closes and another opens.

A wrongful convictions class at the University of Missouri Kansas City Law School will research and investigate my arrest, trial, and appeals this semester. If they deem that I am indeed innocent of the crime, they will decide if there is anything they can do to help. Most all the assisted men in the Innocence Project have used DNA evidence.

Do you remember my elderly friend Faye Copeland, who was on death row? She died recently, bless her heart, and the attorneys from that office attended her funeral in Chillicothe. After the service, her attorney Sean O'Brien mentioned my dilemma to Phil. Sean knows of me because I translated legal papers to Faye and I wrote him through the years in an attempt to help Faye with her appeals.

The reason this particular phone number looked familiar is because I've called it before—when Faye was so ill, and everyone was trying to get her out of prison. Phil said I had spoken to his wife, Jill, who is Sean's paralegal. My first thought, when he said that, was that surely his wife had not been incarcerated here. Where else would I meet someone, since I've been locked up since '86? But it turned out that on several occasions, when I phoned their office about Faye's deteriorating physical condition, Jill had taken the message.

As Phil told me about Sean, I thought about the extraordinary nature of their attendance at the funeral of their former client. Their obligation was over. The only reason they took time out of their busy schedules to drive to north Missouri was out of love and respect—to pay homage. That's the kind of people who work with the Midwest Innocence Project.

Phil also made mention of my wide circle of loyal supporters. Hardly a week goes by that he doesn't hear my name. My family and friends keep talking and working to find someone to help us. The dam broke and tears of love and gratitude rolled down my face as he praised my loved ones.

As soon as Phil hung up, I called Gary. He went bonkers, as you can imagine. After I spilled my good news to Gary, I spilled my news to my roomies.

Mickie, who was mid-chew, jumped up, hugged me tightly, and spit peanuts in my freshly washed hair as she sputtered and cried, "Oh, thank God! I knew someone would listen someday! Oh, thank God! I don't want to leave you here. OHHHH!" Everyone on my floor heard Mickie and began shouting "atta girls" down the hall to me.

Tonight at church, the news bubbled out of my smiling mouth. Hugs and genuine blessings were lavished on me, although one old friend commented dryly, "The Innocence Project rejected my application, because they only want to deal with people who have nothing to do with the crime at all. No involvement. I killed my husband, but I'm not as guilty as the prosecutor says I am." Rendered speechless, I thought to myself, "Duh! It's called the Innocence Project not the I'm-Not-as-Guilty-as-They-Say Project."

So, there you have it! I have prayed relentlessly to return home someday—but have never dared pray for actual vindication.

February 15, 2004

Dear Marsha,

Sarah, Carrie, and their four beautiful children traveled across the state to see me Friday. Callie and Abbey are both two, Drew will turn one next month, and Megan will be one this May. The two-year-olds pronounce "granny" with a hard "g" and no "r": "Ginny." There's no way to describe how my heart warms and swells when I hear my title pronounced in their sweet, childish voices.

For years I've taken advantage of a program called Story Link. Once a month we're allowed to choose a book, read it on tape, and mail it to one of our children or grandchildren. My kids have tons of them, and the funny part is that the little kids just adore them. In fact, on trips to see me, my books-on-tape are played the whole four hours coming and the four hours going. It's a fantastic program to keep the ties that bind strong between separated family members.

Years ago Jane was doing some voiceover work at the university recording studio. The boys were with her, of course, and probably antsy. After she'd done several retakes, little Jace advised, "Mommy, do it like Granny in one take!"

Callie and Abbey are always very anxious and ready to see me by the time they arrive. My daughters tell me that they race from the prison parking lot to the metal detectors, flipping off their shoes like pros.

Of course, the two girls can get loud while trying simultaneously to tell me their personal adventures. A grim guard ordered them to quiet down. She provided the opportunity to teach the girls some of my newly acquired Shakespeare.

"Do you girls know what to say to a witch to get her to go away?" Callie's eyes widened. "A witch with tangly hair?" Obviously, she had some background in witches. "Yes. You say: Aroint thee, witch!" Aroint is Old English for begone, and the girls parroted it all day, flinging their tiny arms for emphasis.

When it was time to fix dinner, Callie, with an ornery glint in her brown eyes, explained that she and Abbey were lions and only eat lion food. She almost had me, but when I peered into the vending machine and spied Dinty Moore Chicken and Dumplings, I exclaimed, "Yes, Megan, I see it! It's lion food. Wow! When did they start stocking lion food?"

Callie shot me a hard look. Baby Megan in my arms just smiled that clueless baby smile that I adore. Abbey glanced at her cousin nervously with a Laurel and Hardy expression, "What a fine mess you've got us into this time, Ollie!" Ignoring the girls' reluctance, I prepared the dish while chattering about how lucky we were to find an actual lion meal in that machine.

I also had forgotten how difficult it is to perform the simplest task with a fat baby on my hip—one who reaches out with curious fingers. Oooo. My left arm felt like it might break off. But the two lions stood mesmerized.

In case you wonder where my daughters were during all of this, Sarah was buying and preparing Momma food for us in another microwave. Baby Drew snoozed peacefully on Carrie.

After dipping a spoon of the gravy and blowing on it for Abbey, who never eats a heated thing that hasn't been blown on, the girls tried a tiny taste. Lo and behold, they both love lion food! Roar! And I love being a granny.

While playing on the floor of the toy area after our lion meal, Drew climbed precariously on all the play furniture. Monkey boy kept us on our toes—exactly like my Matthew at that age.

Megan crawled to my lap, and when I sang, "Fat bottom girls, they make the rockin' world go 'round," she frowned and pouted up her bottom lip as if her feelings were hurt before she broke into a big, drooling grin.

When advising Callie and Abbey to be good to their mommas, they broke out with Queen Latifah's song from *Chicago*: "When you're good to momma, momma's good to you." What characters.

My nose detected a problem that is common among babies. "Someone has a stinky butt," I announced while eying Megan, who wore the guilty look of a dirty-diapered suspect. Callie sternly admonished, "We don't say butt, Ginny. We say bottom." I felt thoroughly chastised by my pint-sized censor.

When it was time to go, we wrestled coats onto everyone. Callie wore hers backward and liked it that way. Abbey grabbed my hand as we made our way to the big steel exit door, "Come home with us, Ginny, and play in my room."

I gently told her that I couldn't. Abbey bent her knees and tugged my hand insistently toward the door. She leaned over as if indicating we should sneak out, and said, "Like this Ginny, come with me like this," and my battered heart broke once more.

Postscript

On Easter Sunday in 2003, I called my second daughter Sarah's home to talk to the family gathered there for the big Easter feast. I enjoyed a long discussion with my oldest grandson about the letter-compilation project that my family had undertaken. Zach, who was fourteen at the time and a budding editor, made a very good point when he mentioned that he didn't know who the letter recipients were and thought an explanation was in order. I won't go into detail about each person I wrote to, but will describe three of my closest friends:

Marsha is my oldest friend; we met in about third grade. It was at her home that we discovered a layered haircut could be done easily if the girl wanting the cut hung upside down from the swing set bar while the other one, wielding the scissors, stayed on the ground and sawed straight across.

After we graduated from high school and before we went off to different colleges in '67, Marsha and I shared a big adventure. We rode a bus to Pagosa Springs, Colorado, and stayed and played part of that summer at a ranch near Wolf Creek Pass. The pack trip in the mountains across the Continental Divide will forever live in my memory.

Nancy and I met on the school bus in the middle of sixth grade, after my family moved a few miles west to put us in a better school district. She lived just a couple of farms around the bend, and as soon as I saw her sweet face, I loved her.

It turned out that Nancy was allergic to horses, which probably wasn't that much of a problem for her until she met me. I loved to ride my little pinto pony bareback to her house, which was nestled way back in the property at the end of a winding half-mile driveway. I vividly recall securing sweaty Chiquita in the barn, dusting the excess horsehair from my jeans, and waltzing into Nancy's house, which had been a bootleg lodge in the time of Prohibition. As soon as I appeared, her eyes would water, and she'd start a sneezing fit.

Nancy, obviously of Danish descent, began her college career at MU, met a man, attended other colleges to the west with John, married in Alaska, gave birth to beautiful twin girls, moved to rural Minnesota, unloaded the husband, worked as a reporter and a schoolteacher, and raised her two wonderful daughters essentially by herself.

Our daughters used to beg us to tell them again and again about how we were so scared when we started junior high at the big school that we held hands as we scurried down the halls between classes. The kids think that's a hilarious picture—but they never attended a little rural grade school and had to make a tremendous transition at the tender age of twelve. Also, this was long before kids knew anything about homosexuality—or any kind of sexuality. Shoot, we danced with each other at school functions. If we had waited for boys to ask us, we'd have grown roots as wallflowers.

Nancy also flew down to Missouri to be with me and my family through the murder trial. She loved my husband, too, and like me had known him since our junior high days.

Many of the letters were written to my friend, Mary. (Hope this isn't confusing since I also have a sister named Mary.) My husband and I met Mary and her now ex-husband Jack when we bought the lumberyard in 1976. Instantly we bonded—and the fun-loving couple joined our co-ed volleyball team. Their brilliant, handsome son is Sarah's age. Jack and Bill were best friends, so when Bill was murdered, Mary and Jack, who were also traumatized, came to our rescue, helping our little kids and me in countless ways. Mary also testified on my behalf at trial about the inept police procedures and shoddy investigation.

After Bill's death, when the kids and I were struggling financially,

Mary's sweet farmer daddy would leave garden vegetables and a lottery ticket on our front porch periodically. And he never wanted any thanks.

My petite, red-headed, freckle-faced, scrappy Mary labored for many years as a hot-asphalt roller operator. Once we met her coming out of the local IGA, and my kids were taken aback to see Mary in a nice dress and heels. She explained that with the horrid weather that winter, she'd taken a part-time job as a secretary. Unemployment compensation only goes so far. Mary is the kind of gal who rolls up her sleeves and does what has to be done—no matter what. She has true grit.

To find one truly good friend in this life is a miracle, but somehow many wonderful women and men bless my life. And I promise I will never take any of them for granted.

Dear Gary,

    I hope you don't r
do hate them, Stop rea
eat this paper.

    Are you still with
if you despise fan mail.

    OK, if you're still r
handwriting), I just wan
touched by your music.
voice — but you know t
But there is an element n
the lonely, restless, sincere
You probably know that n

fan letters. But if you

right NOW — and

? I bet you are — even

ght?

g (and can decipher my

to know that I was

have a beautiful

— and lots of people do.

sound that conveys

rt of the cowboy.

ddy is a real honest-to-God

Afterword by Aisha Sultan

I first learned about Patty Prewitt's incarceration in 2019 while I was researching the clemency petition backlog in Missouri. A law professor at St. Louis University, John J. Ammann, a founder of Community Coalition for Clemency, sent me a dozen petitions to review.

As a journalist, I look for compelling stories from people whose voices may otherwise not be heard. I had no idea how Patty's story would change my life.

Several things jumped out at me from her petition: a police investigation that failed to collect key evidence or pursue credible leads, a prosecutor who focused heavily on her sexual history, and a pathologist with a record of mistakes providing key evidence in her trial.

As I was uncovering the details surrounding Patty's conviction, the former director of the Missouri Department of Corrections also reached out to me. He wanted to publicly call for her release—something he had never done for a prisoner in the forty years he worked at the DOC.

Hers was the most unusual petition I read. There were so many problems in the State's case that it became clear to me that the standard of "guilt beyond a reasonable doubt" had not been met. Beyond that, Patty had already served more than thirty-three years at that point and had a longer list of accomplishments than most people living free in society.

I wrote an editorial in the *St. Louis Post-Dispatch*, where I've worked as a journalist for nearly three decades, making the case for then-Governor Mike Parson to grant Patty clemency. I wasn't hopeful that anything would come of it. State legislators and Patty's adult children had been begging for her release for years. Not a single governor had taken action on her petition.

After I interviewed Patty's attorney, he connected me to her eldest child—her daughter, Jane. She had lost her father as a teenager and had been fighting for her mother's release for decades. She visited her mom every month in prison. I was fascinated by how they had sustained such a deep relationship despite the decades of physical separation and imprisonment. Jane's fierce dedication to her mother, her vulnerability in sharing the most traumatic moments in her life, and her openness to trust me with their story stayed with me long after I filed my editorial.

I'm ashamed to admit that before I met Jane, I was like most Americans who don't think much about people who are incarcerated. Our society assumes that those serving lengthy prison sentences are a danger to the rest of us and deserve to be locked up. I had never personally known someone convicted of murder. It wasn't until I started learning more about Patty's children and grandchildren that I began to understand how entire generations in a family are affected when a mother is incarcerated.

I didn't realize that America has been locking up more mothers than any other place on earth and the devastating ripple effects of these policies.

The more I got to know about Patty—from her children, childhood friends, fellow inmates, and advocates—the more I realized how extraordinary her story was. If her claim of innocence was true, as she had steadfastly claimed since the beginning, then she had suffered every imaginable tragedy. She had been raped more than once. Her husband was killed next to her in their bed. She was unjustly sentenced to fifty years in prison for his murder. She was separated from her five young children. Her son died while she was incarcerated.

How many tragedies can a person bear, I wondered. Even more perplexing to me was Patty's response to her circumstances. She had spent her thirty-eight years in prison learning, mentoring, growing, creating, and helping. So many formerly incarcerated women told me how Patty was the mom they needed while they were in prison. She became the living epitome of blooming where you are planted—even if that's a concrete cell block.

The question that nagged at me was how she maintained hope, a sense of curiosity, a desire to improve herself, and a commitment to giving back despite the injustices she had suffered.

Even though I had never made a documentary before, I decided I needed to tell Jane and Patty's stories in a way that brought people into their worlds. I wanted to give audiences a window into an unfamiliar world through the enduring bond between mother and daughter.

Ultimately, I wanted the audience to decide whether it served the cause of justice to keep Patty imprisoned any longer.

I started applying for grants and entering pitch contests to try to raise the money I would need to hire a crew to make a documentary. I learned how to direct and produce on the fly and with the help of seasoned professionals, who also believed in clemency for Patty.

Whenever anyone asked me why I wanted to make the film, I had one answer: I did not want Patty to die in prison. She deserved to spend whatever years she had left free and with her family, who longed to be reunited with her. We shot dozens of interviews, accompanied Jane on a prison visit to see her mom, and incorporated crime scene footage that police had recorded after Bill's murder. We dug into court transcripts and historical archives, found old newspaper articles on microfiche, and visited the family's original home in Holden, Missouri, and the courthouse in Sedalia, where the trial took place.

I wanted people who watched the film to get to know Patty and Jane as survivors, not statistics. The most moving experience for me was when I interviewed Patty in prison about everything she had experienced, including her most traumatic memories. I could see her reliving the trauma while she described the scenes on camera. I wept while she talked about the rape and finding Bill's bleeding body in the bed.

I knew that once people heard about all the problems in her conviction and all the good she had done behind bars, they too would advocate for her release. During my interviews with Jane, she shared her fantasy of what it would be like when her mother was freed. The scene she described I envisioned in my mind.

That was our goal. That was the vision that kept us going.

We planned a multicity film festival run, beginning with a

premiere in New York, then screenings for state legislators, and multiple public discussions. The documentary, *33 and Counting*, was set to premiere in March 2020. A week before the date, the country shutdown due to the global COVID-19 pandemic.

The film was never shown in a theater although it aired on our local PBS channel and won awards at festivals that all shifted to online screenings. Many people wrote letters and made calls to the governor on Patty's behalf after seeing the documentary. Still, it felt like I had created another heartbreaking disappointment for Patty.

Despite all my efforts, the pandemic prevented us from gaining the momentum around the documentary that I had planned. We couldn't land a distributor, and I worried whether Patty would survive the COVID-19 virus that was running rampant in prisons.

As she has through every hardship she's faced, Patty survived. We stayed in touch, and I continued to write about her case. I tried to help other writers and podcasters who were interested in sharing her story.

In December 2024, I put our documentary on a video on-demand site, askfilmproductions.vhx.tv, hoping to stir interest in her case before Governor Parson left office. I was visiting my family in Texas for the holidays when I got a phone call from a colleague at work.

He asked me if I had heard the news: the governor had granted Patty clemency.

I stopped dead in my tracks. Could this be true? I asked him to send me the press release. I had to see it for myself. I texted Patty's lawyer, who confirmed it was true.

For years, I had prayed this day might come, but to be honest, I had been losing hope.

That day I sent Jane a text congratulating her for a moment she had dreamed about for decades.

At long last, Patty was free.

Aisha Sultan is a syndicated columnist, journalist, and filmmaker.

Photographs from Patty Prewitt's Collection

Wedding Day, Patty and Bill,
August 8, 1968

PATRICIA ANN SLAUGHTER

Engaged

Mr. and Mrs. W. Frank Slaughter have announced the engagement of their daughter, Patricia Ann Slaughter, to William Edward Prewitt, son of Mr. and Mrs. W. K. Prewitt. Both are 1967 graduates of Lee's Summit Senior High School, and are presently attending Central Missouri State College at Warrensburg, Mo. Wedding plans are indefinite.

Lee's Summit Journal,
March 7, 1968

Bill and Patty, December 18, 1970

1979

Happy Holidays
Come & see us!
Love,
Bill, Patty, Jonie
Sarah, Matt, Carrie
& Morgan

Christmas 1979

First Christmas without our dad, 1984

Graduation from Platte Junior College. Patty with
all her children and nephews Jesse and Justin, 1987

William Matthew Prewitt,
age 17, 1990

Sarah, Matt, Carrie, Morgan, Patty, Zach, Jane,
and Jace, Easter 1992

Jane, Zach, Sarah, Patty, Morgan, Carrie,
and Jace, 1995

Jane, Sarah, Patty, Zach, and Jace, 1998

Abbey, Megan, and Patty, 2003

Ann (Mom), Patty, and Frank (Dad), 2003

Patty and Gary, 2003

Acknowledgments

Besides my former farm girls Marsha Frantsen Kearns, Nancy Knudsen Besse, and Mary Stevens O'Roark Englert, I also want to express appreciation to all the kind family, friends, and others who made my survival possible, including but not limited to, and not in any particular order:

Daddy and Momma, aka Wesley Frank and Edith Ann Slaughter; Mary and Doug Longaker, Jesse, Justin; Frank and Brenda Slaughter, Frankie, Betsy, Katie, Jenna, Laura, Amanda; Sarah, Abbey, Megan, Will; Tom, Carrie, Callie, Drew; Jane, John, Zachary, Jace; Morgan, Crystal, Patrick, Alyssa, Matthew; Gary, Frank, Venetta Kirkland; Uncle Ivan, Aunt Marge, Stan, Yvonne; Granny and Grandpa Snow; Grandma and Grandpa Slaughter; Uncle Joe and Aunt Jean; Mother Squires; Jerri and Paul Austin; Nancy's twins Carli and Heather, and Tom.

Aunt Pearl, Don, Fred, Carolyn, Glen, Joyce, and crew; Uncle Russ and Aunt Laura Snow; Uncle Casey; Dot Prewitt; Jim Davis; Harvey, Eunice, Randy; Bob and Jan Eagleson; Luz Cardona, Cesar; Kathy Perkins; Will and Vi Knudsen; Tom, Linda Williams and clan; Ira Griffin; Sally Frantsen; Jim Brown and crew; Linda McBride; Sue Pikey; Pamela Kline; Jim Rutter; Clyde Lamp.

George Lombardi; Gloria and Paul Shy; Mickie Perry; Philip Cardarella; Bob Beaird; Deleta Williams; Dale and Marilou Whiteside; Helen Martin; Residents Encounter Christ; William Edward "Bill" Prewitt; Vicky Riback Wilson; Hugh Francis and Seamus Behan; Michelle Dale and David; Julian and Nellie Jackson; Norma Streumph; Jimmy and Rosalynn Carter; Sue Shear; Father Lou Dorn; Agnes and Bob Wilcox; Rachel Tibbetts; Major Turner; Bryan Goeke; Daniel Kohl; J. Malcolm Garcia; Beth Charlebois; Barbara Baumgartner; Sean and Quinn O'Brien; Ruth Beamer; Cindy Ostmann; Mel and Jean Carnahan; Kevin Windhauser and all the Washington University professors involved in their Prison Education Project.

Peter DeSimone; J. R. Hines; Doc Ayler; Opal and Mike Beard; George Sample; Doris and Glenn Macha; Diane Hannah; Joe and Mike Englert; Brian Banks; Lonnie Coombs; Dave Parker; Jim Phillips; Alex Peebles; Sue Stewart; Mary Schrock; Ruth Slaughter; Bina Davis; Jaye Wright; Jenee Lowe; Marguerite Taylor; Shamed Dogan; Donna Baringer; Jason Flom; Dr. Phil McGraw; Alec Rosenbloom; Dan Martin; Maggie Freleng; Stephanie Granader; Paige Bridgens; John Burnett; Lisa Boyd; Maureen Gorsuch; Hedy Harden; Jeff Humfeld; Laura Phillips; Siobhan Walsh.

Brian Reichart; Jane Aiken; Greg Zlotnick; Tracy McCreery; Barbara Wall Fraser; Marcia McConville and family; D. J. Allen; Angie Ricono; Tony Messenger; Bill Deeken; Sister Monica; Bill Kenney; Quincy Troupe; Story Link; Bill Boucher; Marilynn Haselhorst; Nancy Bolin; Linda Walker; Theresa Harrigan, Patty and Sheena; Aisha Sultan; Elizabeth Townsend; Seth Gordon; Jamie Tomek; Jane Ponte; Lucy Freeman; Amy Sherrill; Cliff and Pat Gustin and family; Juanita Stephens and children; Dr. Joe Kayser and Margie; Harry Wiggins; June Pearse; Rev. Pat Kelley; Beth Long; Rob and Paula McCurren; Julie and Rod Lentz; Denis Shine; Maria Goeliner.

Some People Press would like to thank the following people:
Lakshmi and Hari Cianculli, Jay Platt, Marcy Freedman, Josh Donen, Chris Johanson, Miranda July, Beatrice Red Star Fletcher, Sarah Minnick, Lindy Laurence (from Rational Unicorn), Constance Debré, Kristi Garced, Gretchen Dykstra, J. Malcolm Garcia, Barbara Baumgartner, Elizabeth Charlebois, Aisha Sultan, and the Prewitt family.

About the Author

Patty Prewitt was born and raised on a cattle ranch near Lone Jack, Missouri. Her writing was first published, in *Wee Wisdom* magazine, when she was in second grade. During her incarceration, she won a PEN America writing contest and had both prose and poetry published in *Wrath-Bearing Tree*, the *Massachusetts Review*, *Tampa Review*, *Tacenda Magazine*, *Cholla Needles*, *MiPOesias*, and *Duende*. Two of her plays have been performed at the John F. Kennedy Center for the Performing Arts in Washington, DC. In December 2024, Prewitt was released from prison at age seventy-five, nearly forty years after what she continues to maintain was a wrongful conviction. She resides in Greenwood, Missouri, with family.

About Some People Press

Some People Press publishes autobiographies by formerly incarcerated writers, as well as books on art and other subjects. We challenge the idea that only certain people—with the right education, experiences, and connections—can be published authors. Instead, we encourage writers to use their existing skills and to write about what they know best, their own lives. All profits from sales of autobiographies are split evenly between the Press and the author. Some People Press is supported by book sales and contributions via Venmo @somepeoplepress.

Other books published by Some People Press

Hi Friend by Jess Hilliard

Smile Now, Cry Later by Terry James

Worth It! by Joey Lucero

How Long Is Five Minutes? by Arron Magar

The Blacksmith by Juliano Miller

untitled (Plaid Pantry) by David Rosenak

www.ingramcontent.com/pod-product-compliance
Lightning Source LLC
Chambersburg PA
CBHW020232130626
46549CB00005B/1859